FLORIDA STATE
UNIVERSITY LIBRARIES

JUL 2 2001

TALLAHASSEE, FLORIDA

INTO THE MELTING POT

Into the Melting Pot

Teaching Women's Studies in the New Millennium

Edited by
FIONA MONTGOMERY
CHRISTINE COLLETTE

Ashgate
Aldershot · Brookfield USA · Singapore · Sydney

© F. Montgomery and C. Collette 1997

All rights reserved. No part of this publication may be reproduced, stored in a retrieval system, or transmitted in any form or by any means, electronic, mechanical, photocopying, recording or otherwise without the prior permission of the publisher.

Published by
Ashgate Publishing Ltd
Gower House
Croft Road
Aldershot
Hants GU11 3HR
England

Ashgate Publishing Company
Old Post Road
Brookfield
Vermont 05036
USA

British Library Cataloguing in Publication Data

Into the melting pot : teaching women's studies in the new
    millennium
    1.Women's studies
    I. Montgomery, Fiona II.Collette, Christine
    305.4'2'071

Library of Congress Catalog Card Number: 97-73410

ISBN 1 85972 557 0

Printed and bound by Athenaeum Press, Ltd.,
Gateshead, Tyne & Wear.

Contents

Notes on contributors vii
Acknowledgements x

1. Introduction
   Fiona Montgomery and Christine Collette 1
2. Women's experiences: whose knowledge is it?
   Beryl Madoc-Jones 13
3. Changing identities: two years on with Women's Studies
   Maireud Owen 23
4. 'The gift of intelligent rage'
   Sue Graves 33
5. What can tutors and students do to promote egalitarian relationships in the Women's Studies classroom?
   Penny Welch 39
6. Women's Studies in Human Geography
   David A. Halsall 49
7. Women's Studies/Media Studies changing perspectives: a case study
   Angela Thew and Carol Poole 67
8. 'Exiting the symbols' A discussion of the role and practice of Drama in the teaching of Women's Studies
   Elizabeth Hare 77
9. Reflections of a Black woman reflecting
   Philomena Carlotta Hilaria Harrison 87
10. Agenda for Women's Studies in the context of cultural diversity issues
    Sneh Shah 97
11. Teaching Women's Studies in women's prisons
    Shauna Morton 107
12. Women's Studies in Continuing Education: the Sussex experience
    Gerry Holloway 117

13.	Window on the Netherlands *Greet Goverde*	125
14.	Globalising the 'gender agenda': a critical view of liberal Feminism in the post-Beijing order *Jenny Clegg*	137
15.	Conclusion *Fiona Montgomery and Christine Collette*	153

Bibliography 155
Subject index 167

Notes on Contributors

Jenny Clegg, B.A., Ph.D., Senior Lecturer in African and Asian Studies at Edge Hill University College. Her research interests centre on Third World politics, particularly China, women and development and the Chinese in Britain. She is author of *Fu Manchu and the 'Yellow Peril': the Marking of a Racist Myth,* and has also published articles on women's issues.
Christine Collette, B.A., M.Litt., D.M.A., Senior Lecturer, Women's Studies, Edge Hill University College. Executive member, Society for the Study of Labour History. Teaching and research interests centre around issues of gender, class and ethnicity, including contribution to the New Dictionary of National Biography. Recent publications include: 'Ernest Bevin and Edo Fimmen' and (with Bob Reinalda) 'ITF and women during the inter-war period' in Bob Reinalda (ed.), *The Fimmen Years*, Stichting beheer IISG, Amsterdam; (1996), with Fiona Montgomery, 'The Patience of a Saint and the Cunning of the Devil: Teaching Women's Studies in the 1990s', *Teaching in Higher Education* 1(1); (1995), 'Daughter of the Newer Eve' in Jim Fyrth (ed.), *Culture and Society in Labour Britain*, Lawrence and Wishart, London; (1993), 'Gender and Class in the Labour and Socialist International, 1923-1939', Gabriella Hauch, *Geschlecht, Klasse, Ethnizitat*, Vienna. To be published in 1997, *The International Faith: the British Labour Movement and Europe*, Scolar Press.
Greet Goverde teaches English at Nijmegen Community College. She is involved in local women's and ethnic groupings, politics and is a Green party activist.
Sue Graves is a mature student at Edge Hill University College and Lecturer in Administration at Skelmersdale College.
David A. Halsall, B.A., Ph.D., Senior Lecturer in Human Geography, Edge Hill University College. His interests include Feminist Geography, Transport Studies, the urban environment and the Netherlands, and he has published in a variety of these areas.

Elizabeth Hare, B.A., Ph.D., Head of Drama, Edge Hill University College, Previous publications include work on Educational Drama, Drama and Disability, and the assessment of creative work. Current research interests focus on performance and cultural identity.

Philomena Carlotta Hilaria Harrison, B.Sc., Dip. Psychiatric Social Work, Senior Lecturer at Liverpool John Moores University. Particular interests are issues of racial identity around Black children.

Gerry Holloway is a feminist historian and Lecturer in Women's Studies at the Centre for Continuing Education, University of Sussex. Recent publications include: (with Patricia Ambrose and Graham Mayhew), (1994), *All Change! Accreditation as a Challenge to Adult Education*; two essays in Mary Stuart and Alistair Thompson (eds.), (1995), *Engaging with Difference: the Other in Adult Education.* Forthcoming publications are: 'Finding a Voice: on Becoming a Working-Class Feminist Academic', in P. Mahoney and C. Zmroczek (eds.); *Class Matters*; 'Ada Nield Chew: An Uncomfortable Feminist', in E. Yeo (ed.), *Mary Wollstonecraft: 200 Years of Feminism* and '"Let the Women be Alive!": The Construction of the Married Working Woman in the Industrial Women's Movement, 1890-1914' in E. Yeo (ed.), *Radical Femininities.*

Beryl Madoc-Jones, M.A., Ph.D., Head of Women's Studies at Roehampton Institute. She is co-author with Jennifer Coates of (1996), *An Introduction to Women's Studies*, Blackwell.

Fiona Montgomery, M.A., Ph.D., Head of Women's Studies, Edge Hill University College. She has had previous teaching experience at the Universities of Glasgow, Dundee, Aberdeen and Bolton Institute. Her research interests centre around issues of gender, education, politics, and literature, both in an historical and contemporary setting. Recent publications include: (1995), 'Women Who Dids' in C.J. Parker, *Gender and Sexuality in Victorian England,* Scolar Press; 'Gender and Suffrage: the Manchester Men's League for Women's Suffrage', *Bulletin of John Rylands University Library Manchester*; with Christine Collette (1996), 'The Patience of a Saint and the Cunning of the Devil: Teaching Women's Studies in the 1990s', *Teaching in Higher Education* 1 (1). Forthcoming, (1997) *Edge Hill University College: a History 1885-1997* Philimore Press.

Shauna Morton, B.A., is a Ph.D. student at Sheffield Hallam University. Her research examines the ideology of education in women's prisons. She has taught Women's Studies in a variety of settings including university, community education centres and women's prisons.

Mairead Owen, B.A., Ph.D., Senior Lecturer/Programme Leader in Women's Studies, Liverpool John Moores University. Recent publications include: (1994), 'Commonality and Difference: Theory and Practice', in S. Davies et al. (eds.), *Changing the Subject: Women in Higher Education*; (1996), with M. Price, 'Sitting Pretty: Women's Studies and the Higher Education Community' in J. Elliott et al. (eds.), *Communities and their Universities: The Challenge of Lifelong Learning.*

Carol Poole spent her early years in Libya where she helped set up the Department of Urban Planning at the university of Gayaries. She organised the international conference, Green Towns and Cities UK/USA 1984 and contributed to the report which has subsequently been influential in the urban debate. Her main academic interest has been the development of courses for women and the Black community in Liverpool.

Sneh Shah, B.A., M.A., Ph.D., F.R.S.A., Director of the Centre for Equality Issues in Education, University of Hertfordshire. Editor of *New Era in Education*. Recent publications include: (1996), *Going for Higher Education: A Guide for Refugees and Asylum Seekers.*

Angela Thew, Head of Communication Studies at Edge Hill University College. She has worked in both radio and television. She has particular interest in the role of the media, Latin America, regulation/policy issues of national and international media systems and the British Documentary Movement. Publications include *Somos Mas - Women in Chile under Pinoclet, Mass Media as a Form of Dependency in Latin America* and, in preparation, *The Theory and Practice of Radio.*

Penny Welch, B.A., Senior Lecturer in Politics and Women's Studies at the University of Wolverhampton. Her previous publications include 'Is a Feminist Pedagogy Possible?', in S. Davies et al. (eds.), (1994), *Changing the Subject: Women in Higher Education*, Taylor and Francis.

Acknowledgements

Thanks are due to Julia Hedley for producing such excellent camera-ready copy, Judith Briggs for preliminary typing, Edge Hill University College for small research grants, John Simons for encouragement, Maureen Richardson for help in chasing down references, Greet Goverde and Catharina Bongaerts-Wijnands for providing hospitality in the Netherlands, the Women's Studies Departments of the Universities of Utrecht and Nijmegen, the Geographical Association for permission to use the cartoons and captions in Chapter 6 and Matthew and Luke for 'well-ace' forbearance.

Fiona Montgomery
Christine Collette

April 1997

1 Introduction

Fiona Montgomery and Christine Collette

A melting pot is not a comfortable place. There is excitement and creation but also pain and destruction. The intention is to transform the ingredients into something new. We view Women's Studies as a melting pot; not only the academic traditions, but also cherished instances of past Feminism are thrown in to cook. It is the variety of Women's Studies students, teachers and courses that has heated up the pot and in this book we have collected some of these different aspects of Women's Studies for inspection. It has been justly observed that more has been written about epistemology than about methodology or method of Feminist research (Maynard, 1994). The same is true of Women's Studies teaching so that there is a lack of focus on actual practice. The approach of a new millennium seems a fitting opportunity to discuss ideas about Women's Studies - a discipline which has been developing for thirty years - to debate what has worked and what has not, to try to diminish feelings of isolation and to determine the future character of the discipline.

Into the Melting Pot provides an extensive discussion of teaching practices and chapters dealing with the diversity of women's experiences and the forms of Women's Studies. Contributors 'speak their place' as Women's Studies teachers. They share experiences, enquiring how to develop and sustain an appropriate Women's Studies pedagogy, one which is sensitive to class, ethnicity and sexual orientation, and which responds to the move towards widening access which characterises the current market-oriented education system. They engage with the major work of both reconceptualising academic disciplines and evolving appropriate teaching practices. This includes struggle with the existing 'establishment'. *Into the Melting Pot* therefore brings to life both the excitement and the disappointment of the subject, the joys and horrors of Women's Studies.

In this introduction, the place of Women's Studies within the academy, the student, the teacher and the course are considered. Each contributor's major theme is then outlined. We have edited each chapter, but not sought to change viewpoints or influence conclusions. We are concerned that each contributor does indeed 'speak her/his place'. The final chapter synthesises common themes and will, we hope, be of use in inspiring further discussion of Women's Studies pedagogy, a debate which is vital to the development of this revolutionary philosophy.

Women's Studies in the academy

It is a function of Women's Studies to differ from and challenge mainstream/malestream academic tradition. It is, not surprisingly, perceived as a threat and arouses hostility:

> The Field of "Women's Studies" is the most significant female innovation since the brassière, than which it is impressively more elastic. It stretches all the way from respectable scholarship to a tendentious brand of knitting substitute which serves largely to keep its practitioners out of mischief. Mere allegiance to one's own chromosomes may be a flagrant abdication of intellect, but gender-nonsense still spins money (*Telegraph*, 9 December 1995).

These criticisms deserve an answer, not because of deference to the male tradition, but in order to clarify for ourselves the position of Women's Studies. There are three thrusts to the attack above: first, that Women's Studies has no structure or coherence; second, that it is a device which distances its practitioners from the Woman's Movement; third, that 'gender-nonsense' is highly marketable. Each challenge is answered below.

Structure

There is a structure to the emergent Feminist academic network, but it is an unusual one, which we have sought to illustrate by our choice of contributor. While Feminist blocs in traditional courses are extant, a variety of multi-disciplinary Women's Studies course have effloresced. This was not an inevitable route for Feminist scholarship but has proved reasonably popular with students and within institutions, whose market-driven modular approach has been able to accommodate multi-disciplinary courses. Women's Studies courses fit uncomfortably into the Further, Continuing, Extension, Higher under- and post-graduate scheme of British education and are largely unavailable here at school level. Illustrating this point, a Women's Studies conference session might include women working in prisons, hospitals, with Access students, supervising dissertations with several women working across more than one of these locations. The Women's Studies profile is thus unlike that of other disciplines in that it is both multi-disciplinary and ranges across the education strata. In terms of teaching content and practices, Women's Studies teachers will have more in common with each other, in different locations, than they have with colleagues at their home base.

Relationship to the Women's Movement

There is no doubt that this is problematic. Gerry Holloway's chapter enters the caveat that Continuing Education, because it is more strongly based in the community, has closer links with the Women's Movement than Higher Education. We are aware, however, that some Feminists lament the distance between the Women's Movement and Women's Studies. Others claim that Women's Studies is one facet of the Women's Movement, some that the academy is the last bastion of a movement that has disintegrated. There are problems of definition; the Women's Movement, Feminism and Women's Studies are concepts capable of different understandings. The Women's Movement changes over time and place, as Jenny Clegg's chapter usefully reminds us: 'the Women's Movement in countries such as the US and Britain has become depoliticised, fragmented and institutionalised. But in many developing countries women's activism appears to be on the upsurge'. Feminism has usually been described as action to demand equality for women, while seeking to undermine gender stereotypification and sharing Mary Wollstonecraft's 'wild wish', that physiological difference would cease to have a social, political, or economic meaning.

Diane Elam (Elam, 1994) has, perhaps made the definitive statement on the connection between Women's Studies and the Women's Movement. She cautions that: 'once you know what "feminism" and "deconstruction" are then their political work is done'(p.4). She points to the energy created by the fact that Women's Studies is more than Feminism, as Feminism is more than Women's Studies and may, indeed, be found in other sites within the academy. Thus *Into the Melting Pot* contains chapters from practitioners in Drama, Geography, Communications and Afro-Asian Studies. However, Elam is of the opinion that: 'one of the practical effects of feminism has been the development of multi-disciplinary programmes in Women's Studies' (p.11), although this 'may suggest ... a disciplinary uncertainty and may run the danger of introducing its own oppressive regularities or ambiguity' (p.102). Again, *Into the Melting Pot* addresses the latter points. It is instructive to watch the development of Men's Studies, which as Victoria Robinson (1996, p.110) has written, 'accommodate a problematising of masculinity'.

Discussion of the future of Women's Studies will necessarily involve reflection on Feminisms and the Woman's Movement: the task of reconceptualisation of scholarship which Women's Studies demands involves assessing past Feminisms. Consider, for instance, two recent statements: (Smart, 1995, p.1) 'At its earliest entry into the field of academic work, second wave feminism argued that it is essential to do more than add women into existing frameworks of knowledge and research', and (Gontarczyk-Wesola, 1995, p.66):

Women's Studies, as a feminist pursuit of knowledge, in ideals at least, was never intended to be merely a struggle for equal rights, but a fundamental rethinking of male knowledge and a challenge to its objectivity, impartiality, and neutrality. Furthermore, in the development of Women's Studies, it is also pointed out that the commitment to historical truth and to empowering all women is particularly important.

The Market

Questions of marketability are a difficult issue for Women's Studies practitioners. There is no doubt that there are more women in the academies. In 1991/2 in the under 21 age group, women overtook men for the first time. This move towards equality however, is not reflected in the numbers of women employed in academic posts where men greatly outnumber women: only 265 women out of 4800 people are professors in the 'old' universities; only 92 out of 765 are on grades above principal lecturer in the 'new' universities (*Times Higher*, 24 June 1994, p.13). Furthermore, women tend to receive part-time contracts, stereotypical of women's employment. A lack of full time permanent posts also raises the question of the need to compromise to keep a job. Is it inevitable in patriarchal society that Women's Studies joins the disciplines just when academia is in the doldrums?

On the one hand, market imperatives work in our favour, providing us with our students and our jobs. Universities have 'discovered' Women's Studies much as trades unions have discovered women workers and building societies, women householders. Of course, the need recognised is that of the institutions not the new body of recruits, but, ironically, the discipline has become popular. Recognising our marketability does not mean that we underestimate the difficulties of winning acceptance for Women's Studies and we view this not as a battle once fought and won, but as an ongoing campaign. For instance, Lesbian and Gay Studies are only just gaining credence in Britain: 'it took a tremendous effort to ensure that lesbians and gay men were not just objects of study but could also be objective "studiers"'(Whittle, 1996, p.198).

On the other hand, the market is, after all, a male structure; competition and the profit motive, are not traditional Feminist values. While market imperatives are working towards reduction of the distinction between education strata, in themselves signifiers of social class, these strata are still extant. It would be ingenuous to claim that the distinction between Higher, Continuing and Further Education in Britain was without impact. The demands and rewards of our different locations vary enormously. We have yet to tackle the implications of this; to acknowledge the real impact of these divisions in our lives; to struggle against the class-biased hierarchy they represent; the effect of the values attached to the different levels and the implications for their students; the meanings in terms of gender, ethnic and class bias. This is the classic trap: 'It is a dilemma that all radical political movements face, namely the problem of challenging a form of power without accepting its own terms of reference and hence losing the battle.'(Smart, 1995, p.5).

For instance, we need to acknowledge that work with women returners on Access courses and with mixed Liberal Studies groups are equally demanding but differently rewarded and valued. The former might require more preparation and the latter more survival skills, with a mix in the middle, but such arguments are both problematic and relational. One cannot be a Feminist in one situation but not others; nor sensitive to issues of gender, 'race' and class merely at given times. Feminists have questioned the divisions in education 'for an elite few who have the privileges of directive knowledge, and vocational training for the rest enriched with watered-down doses of "culture"' (Nye, 1994, p.89). By unproblematically accepting our location in one education stratum, we maintain patriarchal market divisions.

Even when Women's Studies is established, we cannot expect a system governed by patriarchy and capitalism to nurture our discipline. Andrea Nye (1994, p.xvi) has cautioned us: 'if civilisation is male in its very constitutive structure, there is no mechanism for women's thoughts but men's thoughts; revised, corrected, but still categories, methods, arguments borrowed from men'. Traditional subjects close ranks, timetabling takes place without acknowledging the needs of mature students. Even calling our subject 'Women's Studies; causes problems since being at the end of the alphabet often means we are missed off lists, do not appear on publicity or receive a poor deal in timetabling because 'we haven't got to "w" yet'. Shauna Morton writes of hiding Women's Studies under the guise of 'Introduction to Sociology', having rejected the neutral 'Gender Studies'. The need to campaign continuously for ourselves as women is destructive of our space in two ways, first by demanding the spending of our energy and second, by blocking developments beyond those of Feminist 'standpoint' theory; thus, arguing for Queer theory, Whittle (1996, p.203) writes that radical lesbian separatists in the first wave of the Feminist challenge to the academy 'were locked into a process of explanation, then deconstruction of gender difference rather than reconstruction of theory'. We are asked for loyalty not to the discipline or academia in general, but to the institution. Marketing has become everyone's responsibility. Without our support, income is not generated, there can be no teaching. There is a complexity of expectations to meet; management; administration; student: it is a buyers' market.

The student

If Women's Studies courses operate across the market divides of education, there is, equally, no such thing as the typical Women's Studies student. Nor do we seek, like latter-day Frankensteins, to create such a creature. Rather we wish to provide opportunities for women of all kinds, to include, not exclude. The diversity of Women's Studies students (partly natural to the discipline but also encouraged by market need to recruit widely) demands a Feminist, empowering approach. This causes Penny Welch to examine how egalitarian relationships can be promoted in the Women's Studies classroom. Of mixed 'race' and ethnicity, class, sexual orientation, many of our students are mature, most are women, nearly all are able-bodied.

Kelly Coate Bignell (1996) cites the HMS 1993 Survey, that most students on Women's Studies programmes are female, white, aged between 30 and 50. Some students are mothers, some newly learning sexual experiences, heterosexual and lesbian, some living on their own, others with partners male and female. Mairead Owen in her chapter cites a lesbian student whose comment on her fellow heterosexual students was, 'they're just from a different planet to me'. Some students have experienced homelessness and residence in refuges. Some are socially adept, others not. Being Black in an overwhelmingly White environment can lead to isolation, the need to survive taking over from the desire to devote oneself to studies; we are convinced this leads many Black students to underachieve. Some have worked/are working: a thirty-six hour working week outside the academy is not uncommon. Some students have taken on stereotypical women's low paid, casual service labour *because* they are following the Women's Studies course part-time. What of class? We do not want to put working-class women in a position where they no longer appreciate the forces and institutions which have shaped their lives; this would be disempowering. It is important to acknowledge connections to the past. All of these things impact on our course.

Like Kelly Coate Bignell, some contributors, including Mairead Owen and Greet Goverde have researched their own students. Others, for instance David Halsall, carry out similar research indirectly through student evaluation of the course. We have preferred to give space to a student to speak directly: as Coate Bignell writes (1996, p.316), 'the inclusion of student voices in published research seems to be a logical extension of feminist pedagogical practice'. Sue Graves' chapter is eloquent of the penalties and rewards of a Women's Studies student. We are well aware that it is 'easy to appeal to the emotions and naive idealism of undergraduates, thus making them feel "empowered" and "connected"', when the reality is very different. (Koertge and Patai, 1995). Empowering means giving space to student experiences but not forcing them to share these with us, since we have our own baggage in tow. It is important that our students are equipped to deal with the academy on its own terms; that they learn proper academic conventions so that they can compete on equal terms with those from more established subjects; and thus be in a position to initiate change. This removes the charge that Feminist pedagogy 'deskills' students. It does not imply or involve 'selling out'; on the contrary, it challenges oppression within the academy. Taking the standpoint of a working-class woman, Tamsin Wilton (1995, p. ix) insists:

> I am made deeply uneasy by those feminists who reject the academic enterprise as inherently patriarchal. To me that makes about as much sense as saying that women should not learn how to fix cars because technology is inherently patriarchal. *Nothing* is inherently masculine/feminine or inherently patriarchal.

And,

> The academy is rife with oppressive practices because (its practices) is not just about learning, it is about gate-keeping and reputation, jumping through hoops and collecting letters after your name. But you can refuse to play these games. You can demistify jargon, widen access to and understanding of specialist language ... refusing to engage with theory at any but the most basic level colludes with our own oppression (p.x).

Mairead Owen relates how teaching students academic conventions enabled a student to appreciate that broadsheet newspapers now spoke her 'language'. Several contributors express the inability of teachers to meet student expectations because these are both limitless and contradictory. Meanwhile institutions are under-funded and resources are only too finite. Chapters repeatedly remark on the way that students change; Shauna Morton for instance, explicitly made space for student transformation.

The teacher

Such evidence of change in students raises the role of the teacher. What are the constraints and opportunities for us, teaching Women's Studies? At the end of the day the student will be assessed by the teacher, assessment which has to stand up to rigorous scrutiny. This involves a degree of control no matter how non-authoritarian we might wish to be. This dilemma was especially keen for Shauna Morton in relation to women prisoners. The editors are fortunate in addressing students who, largely, accept the learning situation; other colleagues may have groups coerced into education by unemployment or the requirements of the social security system. To what extent should we require attendance at seminars; accept excuses for late submission of work; engage in understanding child care problems? We want to distance ourselves from the implications of the teacher's aloofness and superiority that were inherent in some of our past experiences (such as standing on dais in a position of command over students who were referred to by title and surname) but we remain, necessarily, figures of authority. Penny Welch points to the danger of thinking we are egalitarian when we are only exercising power in a different way. We recognise the paradox of which Fuss (1990, p.13) wrote, that Feminist academics 'invest their career in the battle to validate "female experience"' while classroom practice privileges those 'in the know' and reduces teacher and student to identity labels which have hierarchies. Some Feminists have envied their male colleagues' freedom from such worries, (Flax, 1990, p.45) although there are enlightened men who are aware of the oppressive nature of the academy and the effects this can have on women's health (Hobsbawm).

In fact, our power over location and timetable is limited. This, in turn, affects the way we deliver our courses. Meanwhile, our very popularity has its own problems of managing large student groups and is obviously demanding of staff time. Pedagogic techniques, such as the small group, the supportive situation for self-aware learning, are threatened.

We have a responsibility to maintain a high intellectual quality in our lessons, but also to make them accessible. We need to consider our agenda; whether we are using the classroom to campaign. We must not be manipulative. We must be careful about creating ourselves as the 'subject' of our teaching. Opinions differ on how much biography should be included in courses: to Philomena Harrison it is vital to identify herself; Angie Thew and Carol Poole, however, give students their autobiographies 'for what it is worth'. This dilemma is especially keen for us because our modules centre on relationships; Plummer (1995, p.136) has written of the efflorescence of sexual 'story telling' and its impact on the academy: 'Academics ... turn to ... the personal narrative, the play, the poem, the collective story, the chorus': are we joining in this personal narrative explosion, and if so what are the dangers? Liz Hare demonstrates the value of, and interrelatedness of, Drama and Women's Studies. Conversely, we must guard against becoming mechanistic; at our worst moments, we fear that academies are beginning to demand repetitive work; that there is little time to meet and discuss new ideas, offer support, explore responses, so that we suffer from what Simone Weil described as the 'malheur' of female industrial work, where there is 'no time or energy for solidarity, ...simple kindness' so that 'she began to feel a mark on her soul' (Nye, 1994, p.63). Weil thought education and culture could overcome this, but is this true today? One of the aims of *Into the Melting Pot* is simply to offer support in recognition of this problem.

The market operates not only between, but within institutions. As Philomena Harrison writes, 'games of sexism and racism are played out'. Here, affirming our equal rights demands that we reach senior positions in the academy; and this means engaging with the academy on its own terms. The alternative might be that we inhabit a 'women's corner', less respectable academically: Kitzinger (1994) has warned that:

> "Women centred" interaction often translates into the celebration of a purportedly conflict-free zone of female solidarity .... not only does this ideology perpetuate the old stereotype of women as sensitive blossoms unsuited to the cut and thrust of academic debate; it also means the repression of conflict, and the silencing of those who insist on drawing attention to differences of opinion. ... the result is that debate is stultified,

criticism is muted, and conflict is forced underground. We become a self-protective sisterhood, locked into self-congratulatory eulogies of each other's work.

Recent editions of *Gender and Education* (1993, 1995) recommended studying women mentoring to this end (1993) and 'rigorous empirical data on promotion chances, for tighter arguments on discrimination' (1995).

As Women's Studies teachers, how do we perceive success? What hierarchic values do we place on publishing, attending conferences? Again we have to live in the real world, as Ribbens and Edwards (1995, p.49) found with their Women's Workshop on Qualitative Family/Household research:

> The group reluctantly took on a name, becoming the Workshop and we have a co-ordinator. ... an unnamed feminist women researchers' support group could not be cited on CVs or acknowledged in publications, could not be justified in terms of time and resources, without an "official" existence.

We share the problem identified by Kelly, Burton and Regan (1994, p.42) that researchers have 'less financial reward, status and security' than teachers; that there are hidden, secretarial aspects of our job which are undervalued. This raises the difficulty of 'How do we work with one another when our knowledge, experiences and confidences are not equal?'. This speaks also of our position as editors of this book; the desire not to impose our own understandings on our contributors contributes to its eclecticism. Even editorial changes of a minor nature have important philosophical meanings which put us in a position of power that we must question. For instance, in order to standardise we took the decision at the outset to spell Women's Studies with capital initial letters: we therefore followed suit with, for instance, Cultural Studies or Drama. We have also preferred 'Black' and 'White' with initial capitals, although our Black contributors did not always do so. We have tried to be careful not to lose the original 'voice', but the balancing act is a fine one. Clearing space for ourselves to do this meant using personal time on a research trip: however, like Philomena Harrison we agree with bell hooks that 'Work makes life sweet'.

Women's Studies courses

It is instructive to consider the present plethora and differences of Women's Studies courses. Those in Britain have been informed by three sources: development within a British education system, in which continuing and further education have been important, as we have shown; the American model; and the European model.

Regrettably it is a function of the continuing dominance of patriarchy in British society that we are sometimes distanced from European Community Programmes on Equal Opportunities for Men and Women, 1996-2000 aimed at promoting women's employment and equal opportunities for all, such as HORIZON, ADAPT, INTEGRA, NOW. However, in Brussels, the Central Unit for Women's Employment, Equal Opportunities Commission, European Parliament Women's Rights Committee and the European Women's Lobby are active. The European Union has produced a very impressive report stressing the importance of Women's Studies as a force for the integration and harmonisation of the European Community. It also stresses the 'need for stronger European co-ordination and sharing of information about Women's Studies research and education in the European Union' (p.4). We wish briefly to consider here a European model of Women's Studies and its base in the Netherlands, which Greet Goverde's chapter helps set in context. This discussion has been assisted by research trips we have made to the Netherlands; we agree with Greet Goverde's point about the importance of doing, in addition to theorising.

The Women's Studies Centre at Utrecht University has produced a *Report on Women's Studies Activities in Europe for the Commission of the European Union* (1995). Women's Studies International Europe (WISE) is also based at Utrecht. As is claimed in the WISE *European Women's Studies Guide* (Utrecht, 1993): 'the Netherlands is the country of trade, the gateway to the continent. In Women's Studies as well, it has been a point of intersection for different feminist cultures ... the Dutch are traders of thought'. Among issues discussed in the report for the European Commission are women's access to information technology, a Women's Studies dictionary, and links with the Women's Movement. The report rightly states (p.2) 'Women's Studies aim at the transformation of education and university curricula in such a way as to reflect and further the social changes in the status of women'. Thus those dealing with concrete women's issues should perhaps have greater links with academic departments. An example is the Nijmegen International Women's Centre - where part-time and volunteer women work extremely hard to integrate immigrants, many of whom are from Turkey and Morocco, into Dutch society. This is multi-culturalism at grass roots level: each individual's culture is prized and its strengths shared with others. There is however, a great disparity between the situation of women teachers in the adult secondary schools facing cuts and job losses and the academic Women's Studies department who enjoy government funding and government support for Chairs in Women's Studies.

As we have shown, these issues are keenly felt within British Women's Studies. This raises for us the question of the future of Women's Studies: is this just about getting women into the academy? If it is, then change should have taken place, since there are now more women students than men, though not more women academics in senior positions. This indicates that we have made strides forwards, since Women's Studies can be found in most institutions, but change is on the surface, only skin deep. Furthermore, having encouraged women back into education as adult learners, the Academy often denies them (especially working-class women) further access to its upper reaches. The glass ceiling often operates against these women undertaking research and if they do manage it, against all the odds, the next problem is that of getting a job. When academic disciplines display Feminist characteristics, does that mean that they lose credibility within the Academy? What is the role of the Feminist academic? These are questions which can only be resolved by Feminist debate, the Feminism of the present and future. It is again in this area that *Into the Melting Pot* makes its contribution.

Let us consider the experience of our contributors. David Halsall, Elizabeth Hare, Angie Thew and Carol Poole present their experiences in translating Women's Studies into other disciplines. David Halsall describes the problems and rewards of teaching Women's Studies within male-dominated Geography and introduces a further dimension to ideas about the typical student profile by discussing his experiences in trying to educate first year Geographers to the need for a Feminist perspective. Elizabeth Hare demonstrates the benefits and interconnectedness of Drama and Women's Studies. She also points out how challenging a Women's Studies approach is: 'what has happened is that having moved out of the male reality to construct our own, we have moved back into it with our challenge', a challenge which has gained much from lesbianism. Angie Thew and Carole Poole detail the problems of producing a module on 'Women and the Media', noting how the transformation taking place in Women's Studies and Media Studies lead to the re-examination of concepts and methodologies.

These essays are essentially about spreading the 'message'. How is this message received? What do students actually make of Women's Studies? How do they cope with its challenges? Sue Graves, a mature student, tells of the practical difficulties of actually effecting change both in her own life and more generally once the ideas have been assimilated. Her excitement in year one is tempered in year two by her realisation of how little society had changed. Mairead Owen, from the point of view of a tutor, reflects on her student profile, showing the ways in which Women's Studies acts as a melting pot for all who come into contact with it. And Beryl Madoc Jones debates the use of women's experience in the classroom while Penny Welch considers the question of egalitarian relationships between teacher and student.

So far, contributors have tended to concentrate on Higher Education. This however, is only one of the strata in the education system. Gerry Holloway reminds us that Women's Studies developed from the Women's Movement of the 1960s and puts forward the view that Women's Studies has 'maintained stronger links with the Women's Movement' and 'operates as a bridge between the academic world of Women's Studies in HE and the social and political movement'.

Shauna Morton also sees Women's Studies as a bridge and her chapter on 'Teaching Women's Studies in Prisons' explains the subterfuges she had to engage in to secure a 'place' for Women's Studies. Her experience illustrates 'the link between the origins of misrepresentation and public understanding of feminism generally, and Women's Studies in particular'. This is a valuable reminder of the difficulties some women have to encounter in even gaining access to Women's Studies.

Greet Goverde provides a 'Window on the Netherlands' which compares how easy/difficult it is for women in the Netherlands to continue their education. Philomena Harrison writes a personal account of the double burdens of racism and sexism, explaining their relevance to Women's Studies and seeing truthtelling as an important aspect of healing. Sneh Shah also discusses racism within the context of multiculturalism. And Jenny Clegg deals with an issue which will doubtless be of great importance in the new millennium *viz* globalisation of the gender agenda.

2 Women's experiences: whose knowledge is it?

Beryl Madoc-Jones

Teachers and students participating in Women's Studies courses have come to respect women's experiences as an important and valued resource in curriculum design. In the context of the academy, this has meant challenges to main stream (male stream) ways of knowing and doing. Such challenges invoke reactions tinged with unease, not to say suspicion. At the heart of these concerns in the academy about the appropriateness of experience lies anxiety about credibility - couched in a traditional discourse about academic standards.

The use of women's experience in the classroom (as opposed for example, in women's groups, community based) is undeniably problematic and presents its own challenges. This chapter will revisit epistemological debates about experience as valid knowledge; examine pedagogical issues stemming from use of experience and in the process argue foregrounding experience as a curriculum strategy allows the development of similar intellectual and critical skills to those espoused by others engaged in the academy. I hope to demonstrate that reframing the epistemological basis of the curriculum to legitimate experience may enhance rather than undermine the shared goals of members of the academy.

Epistemological Concerns

The history of interest in experience

An interest in and a recognition that experience has had a crucial part to play in Women's Studies came from two major and inter-related sources. One was the Feminist critique of the main Western paradigm of knowledge, which has been dominant since the Enlightenment. This paradigm has been acknowledged as a male paradigm, its epistemological justification rooted in notions of objectivity and rationality. Knowledge construction has been controlled by the scientific canon and has given rise to 'grand theory'. Liz Stanley (1993) has reminded us that this kind of theory seeks to offer abstract universalising understandings of reality, rooted in causal, often mono-causal explanations. This has resulted in forms of abstract knowledge which are not grounded in 'practical lived experience' (Stanley, 1993, p 45). A critical response to this has come through the articulation of a range of Feminist theoretical perspectives. Feminist theorists have shared a perception that social reality for women is experienced as oppressive and that women typically find themselves in an unequal power relation with men. They have sought to identify and construct explanations of this oppression/unequal power relation in the belief that such intellectual enterprises would offer the means to politise that 'knowledge'. In other words it would point the way to strategies for improving women's lives, thus changing women's experiences.

The articulation of a range of Feminist perspectives just referred to, is in itself part of the intellectual climate in Feminist scholarship which has promoted the importance of experience as a curriculum input in the Women's Studies classroom. Although a sense of connectedness and binding commonality stemming from shared membership of a gender category remains a key notion, it has been increasingly recognised that gender is lived in a multiplicity of ways. These are understood to be outcomes of a complex relationship between gender and other aspects of individual identity - for example race/ethnicity, class, age and religion. Gender both unites and divides. While it may be the case that women are linked by a recognition and celebration of womenhood and common oppressions rooted in inequalities associated with their ascribed gender, multiple identities mean that women are in touch with their gender in very different ways. The specific forms of oppression encountered are varied. Documenting experience is an important step in unpacking the significance of difference and understanding (theorising) them.

The second source of interest in experience came from the relationship between the Women's Movement of the post-second World War period and the development of Women's Studies. The Women's Movement, like its sister intellectual movement (Feminisms) also took its inspiration and reason for being from the recognition that women were oppressed. This was its political basis. As a political movement, a prior aim has been to raise consciousness amongst women concerning the nature of these oppressions. This was regarded as facilitating the mobilisation of political will to design strategies to deconstruct the basis of these perceived oppressions. This in turn led to the possibility of change. Fundamental to this process has been going back to where oppression 'happens': the minutiae of everyday experiences. One way in which this has been achieved is through the development of groups in which women could meet to share experiences.

In the ways outlined above, both Feminist intellectuals and activists have drawn much of their inspiration from women's experiences: hence the centrality of experience as a category in the construction of knowledge for and about women in Women's Studies.

The links between theory and experiential knowledge

Experience as an analytic category has entered the Women's Studies curriculum in a number of ways: it is being codified whenever women are making a representation of their direct everyday lives. This happens when women write personal narrative including auto-biography, auto-biographical novels and diaries; when women participate in interviews; when historians engage in oral history and in uncovering written and documentary history; when ethnographic methods make direct observation of women's lives; when women talk in groups, including the arena of the classroom. All recorded experience is historical since it is by definition, what has happened to the individual. It always involves both reconstruction and representation since it invokes a lived experience. Communicating experience to others requires a process of selection/ordering/interpreting. Such a process or set of processes, I would argue (as others have) is a form of theorising. Women's knowledge/understanding derived in this way from confronting experience, begins to acquire an epistemological validity. Its construction triggers intellectual processes which contextualise raw 'experience', identify significance leading to generation of previously unnoticed meaning, becoming understanding.

Acknowledging such intellectual endeavour to be a legitimate form of theorising, overcomes some of the problems inherent in the grand theory approach. The search for 'causal' explanation has been heavily criticised for its seeming inability to provide explanation of the complexity and fragmentation of life as it is lived. Its level of categorisation and generalisation can over-simplify reality and estrange the individual. The search for universal causation can only at best approximate reality and in the process may distort it. Recognising ourselves as experiencing women/men allows us to situate ourselves and begin the process of probing our realities. Initially this may be a quest to find the self as a private construct. When conducted in a public arena like the classroom rather than the private world of the mind, the limitations of an internal reflexive dialogue carried out within oneself as a gateway to reality becomes apparent. Connections with others become essential. This may lead to a re-evaluation of the self as a social construct.

This is an important conceptual leap in order to be able to theorise or understand ourselves rather than the self in isolation. It is at this point that we can begin to identify a relationship between experiential theorising and larger scale theories. A conceptual framework is needed to assist the individual in conceptualising links with others. For example, concepts such as 'institution', 'system' and 'society' or 'power' and 'control' might unlock a way forward. The challenge is to make these links without burying the individual. The point being made here is that working with experience as a recognised epistemological category does not preclude relating this to other more conventional theoretical approaches. This point has been highlighted by Lorraine Code (1989), a Feminist philosopher, when she says that it is important for Feminist epistemology to remain in dialogue with 'male stream' epistemology. The issue is not a wholesale rejection or adoption of established theory but a recognition that there is much there which can assist women in finding creative ways of using it to develop and expand women's knowledge. The intellectual task of becoming familiar with existing theoretical perspectives, Feminist or otherwise, facilitates the establishment of a conceptual framework, an essential step in the pursuit of a capacity for critical thinking and academic creativity.

At stake is the way in which women, either students or teachers/researchers make use of intellectual modes available to them and learn from traditional epistemologies. Liz Stanley (1995) has argued that the tendency inherited from the scientific paradigm to think and conceptualise in terms of binaries - for example objectivity/subjectivity, emotionality/rationality and of course feminine/masculine - has been unhelpful. It gets in the way of gaining epistemological credence and recognition for women's knowledge. She has pointed out that women can and do think rationally about their subjective realities, taking a rational stance when reflecting on the emotional. This can be seen at work with women inside and outside the academy. Liz Stanley (1995) has illustrated this point with an examination of her mother's ability to make sense of traumatic life events (a woman without the opportunities for academic training). An analysis of the coping strategies, both intellectual and emotional, employed by her mother to negotiate and come to terms with the serious illness and loss of her husband led her daughter to argue that there is no necessary divide between thought processes being worked through by academics in a protected situation and similar engagement on the part of those 'outside'.

This challenges notions that only the privileged - members of the academy - have access to attributes and skills deemed crucial for pursuit of knowledge and questions a rigid distinction between scientific and common sense knowledge. The status of scientific knowledge has facilitated academics' 'tendencies to gatekeep' - to privilege certain ways of knowing and epistemologies as if they are exclusive. Exclusivity is then sustained through epistemological control. Power comes from being able to control who has the right to construct knowledge and importantly where it is acknowledged to be done. If similar intellectual processes can be identified the other side of the 'gate' (academic) in the real world of everyday life, then a division between knowledge located in that real world and that generated through similar intellectual procedures in the academy becomes unsustainable. As Liz Stanley (1995, p.192) has said, '... rational thought, critical detachment, analytic theorising ... are not exclusively scientific attributes but rather human ones'.

If women demonstrate analytic potential in their everyday reflective lives, then this intellectual potential is carried into the classroom. With them also comes a wealth of experiential knowledge on which they have already worked and begun to sharpen their intellectual skills. It seems to be a bizarre situation (non-rational?) to demand that one important resource for learning is carried forward while the other, intimately related, is left behind. Working with what is already known and at least partially understood provides a sound pedagogic basis to take students into a challenging intellectual climate in which they will have access to a further range of epistemologies and ways of knowing.

Epistemic responsibility

At the core of epistemological concerns lies the matter of credence and acceptability. Dissatisfaction with the way in which individual experiences have been distanced and isolated from the opportunity for careful scrutiny has led Feminist philosophers to (i) identify, as a key task, the search for acceptable/credible ways of knowing - via experiences - and (ii) to find theoretical positions which would overcome the disjuncture between knowledge codified in traditional disciplines and the knowing arrived at through confronting experience (Code, 1989). Many women (and men for that matter) have come to academic study, particularly in the Social Sciences, motivated by a desire to know themselves better. All too often, students have been dismayed to find that they could not locate themselves in those bodies of knowledge. Lorraine Code (1989) has suggested that a Feminist epistemological project should be to devise responsible ways of knowing which would restore continuity between the realities of experience and theorised exposition of them. This endeavour would take to heart the notion of *epistemic responsibility*, a term developed by her. It involves recognising 'human cognition to be an active process of taking and structuring experience' (Code, 1989, p.160). However this process of making sense of experience is one which needs to be policed: certain conditions ought to be put in place in order to safeguard the integrity of experiential knowledge and its epistemological foundation.

A carefully monitored project of this kind would strengthen the case for experiential knowledge to take its place along with (rather than as an alternative to) long established epistemologies. Cognitive constraints such as distorting influences of stereotypical ideas about women and their nature would find no place in this coming to know. Knowing well requires openness, humility in the sense of recognising what is not known and a willingness to rethink entrenched positions.

The sharing of experience in a social context is made accessible through women talking about their histories with one another. An academic context (classroom) requires that these accounts stand up to epistemological scrutiny. Appropriate personal accounts in this situation are not the outpouring of relatively unmediated experience. It is the case that there are clearly identifiable criteria for discerning 'ultimate truth'. At the same time reflective story-telling in the form of personal accounts should be sufficiently organised or specific that it can lead to the shaping of theory in the sense of understanding. It is an informed understanding of what it is to know reality as a women, putting us in touch with ourselves and each other.

Pedagogic Encounters

The foregoing analysis of epistemological issues arising from the use of experiential knowledge in an academic context has implications for the pedagogy of a Women's Studies curriculum and its delivery. These implications open up a set of pedagogic issues which demand analysis. These stem from the different epistemological criteria from those underpinning knowledge construction in the more familiar Western paradigm, and commitment to scientific modes of intellectual inquiry. The delivery of a Women's Studies curriculum which privileges experiential knowledge obliges teachers and learners to co-operate together to establish pedagogic strategies which will preserve and protect epistemological integrity.

The first issue I want to deal with is the problem of 'experiential authority'. The concept of authority is being used here to denote that events 'happened' rather than claiming some notion of absolute truth. Self revelation is a difficult personal undertaking. Speaking of experience and articulating it is an act that may convey to its 'owner' a sense of significance and authority. This can be very empowering. To some the acknowledgment of experience will come as a sense of relief, should they find that they are not alone in that experience. 'Knowing' that it is shared, brings a sense of validation. This can be a very important step in liberating a woman from a tendency to look inward and locate herself as the cause of her problems or to blame herself (Greed, 1990). Retrieval of often repressed experiences and acknowledgment that they happened validates, and on occasion, may empower.

The concept of validation is one that itself needs addressing. I have already made reference to 'epistemological' validity. Then it was used to signify that recognition of the existence of a phenomenon - in this case 'women's experience' - is essential in order to confer a category or status in epistemology. The retrieval of women's place in psychology, history, sociology or literature is part of the legitimation process validating women's knowledge.

Acknowledgment of women's experience through curriculum space in the classroom or other learning situations enables women participating to gain a sense of personal validation. Finding a voice in a social context and sharing experience confirms that it happened. Sharing means making experience public, however small the size of the participating group. A listening and receiving public group confirms that experience in a number of ways. It recognises that it 'happened' rather render it insignificant through invisibility, marginality or according the ultimate indignity of doubting its veracity. (After all, are not women 'irresponsible', 'unreliable' and 'prone to take liberties with the truth'?) Part of this process of validating experience through women finding and exercising a voice involves according that experience a value - in the eyes of both the individual and those engaged in constructing an epistemologically grounded women's knowledge/studies. The two levels of validation - the personal and the epistemological - proceed side by side. The process of validating experience confers an authority grounded in testimony.

On the other hand, the process of acknowledging experience and its personal significance can be intimidating. Subjectivities and identities are precarious, yet need to be sufficiently intact to take the strain of public scrutiny of a particular kind, in the context of the power structures and academic standards of the academy. There are very real differences between sharing experiences in supportive locations such as consciousness-raising groups and the academic Women's Studies classroom. The classroom as a learning arena is subject to rules of pedagogic procedure set by the complex organisations of which it is a part. Membership of the group (class) has been determined by a common goal - academic achievement and recognition in the form of a qualification which has currency beyond the classroom. The process of acquiring these goals involves an ability to negotiate successfully constraints coming from unequal power structures. Power relations between teacher/learner, older/younger students, or female/male participants, can be very inhibiting if not negotiated successfully. The confidence required to examine critically an element of one's own experience or that of another in the context of unequal power relations, cannot be taken for granted. Rules of engagement and procedure need to be clearly understood, agreed and implemented in the interests of good pedagogy. A clearly understood set of rules needs to be in place and agreed with all classroom participants. At the core of this is a recognition of respect for individual/different voice and right to exercise it, or withhold it. Practical rules of engagement can be agreed for oral discussion, for example always ensuring that one participant takes on a 'chairing' role to make sure that all those wishing to speak out, are given an opportunity.

Speaking out is not always a comfortable situation. Consider the problematic situation of the student who finds herself 'alone' with her experience. She has shared it by talking but finds that it is not shared in the sense of connecting her to others who have had similar experiences. This is a situation which can be disempowering and raises the question of the listening climate of the classroom. I will return to this question later.

A second major issue to be addressed is the question of 'silence'. Not all students want to engage in self revelation in the classroom. Mary Belenky (1986) has referred to silence as an epistemological position. It may reflect a woman's relation to authority and inhibit capacities to develop representational thought, leading to reliance on externally mediated sources of validation of themselves and their experiences. Young students sometimes indicate that their 'experience' is of little value and are intimidated by the 'voice of experience'. In such situations, they are unable to identify with 'subjective knowing' as a source of validation. For example, students can find themselves feeling 'left out' when topics of investigation lie outside their own experience, suffering the isolation of the 'other'. Julia, a first year student made the following comment after a class on mothering: 'I can't connect with it at all, it has nothing to do with where I'm at.'

This led to silence on two counts: offering no reflections from a personal point of view and feeling too inhibited to contribute to discussion on the experiences of others. The student in this case was feeling silenced in two ways. On the one hand, she had nothing which was suitable for personal validation but felt unable to participate in epistemological validation by contributing to analytic comments. It is the responsibility of the teacher to make a student feel comfortable when remaining silent. Silence can be a very positive stance if at the same time respectful listening takes place. In this way silence can be used to support learning.

A related issue is the matter of confidentiality. Classrooms are not intended to be therapeutic environments and I would argue that the rules of confidentiality which govern other professional relationships, such as the religious confessional, the medical consultation, are inappropriate. The classroom is a public arena. It needs to be clearly understood by all participants in the learning situation that once knowledge is shared, it ceases to be private property but is in the public domain and available for public scrutiny according to the canons of epistemological responsibility governing the situation. This means that students should have the right to remain silent and to feel no pressure to place themselves reluctantly in the 'curriculum'. An emphasis on sharing experience can all too easily itself become a form of oppression. Those who do choose to present experience for analysis need to remember that respecting the private is not the same thing as confidentiality and the two should not be confused. A student made the following comment to me recently: 'Strong emphasis on confidentiality stopped contributions recently - risk and underlining the heaviness of that risk became too heavy.' Confidentiality can become a constraint on 'knowing well'.

Dealing with the problem of 'silence' brings the discussion back to a third identified issue, already touched upon, that of listening. Maggie Hum (1991) has used the concept of 'watchful listening'. This suggests a notion of listening as a purposeful and active process which is a form of interaction itself. Listening in this sense facilitates the establishment of empathy in the classroom and helps prepare us for the realisation that what we have thought was purely 'personal', is not in fact so. Listening to others articulating experiences provides the basis for making connections between ourselves and others. This is essential for theorising to being to take place. It provides the conditions for the emergence of what Mary Belenky (1986) called connected knowing. The creation of empathy and connectedness is one way to gain access to other women's knowledge.

The ability to enter other people's knowledge is necessary to take on board a fourth issue in experiential revelation: that of difference. This can make the choice whether to enter the arena or not highly problematic. One of the potential problems of building experience into the classroom knowledge through the process of self revelation is that as much contradiction as confirmation of experience is likely to result. A major challenge for teachers and learners in Women's Studies is to find ways of recognising and respecting diversity in situations in which essentialist notions of membership of a category of 'woman' are not enough. When a woman tosses a piece of herself in the form of self disclosure into the classroom arena, she is doing a number of things; she is deconstructing the binary division between private/public and exposing her personal experience(s) to public scrutiny. This can be very painful. The process of having oneself 'picked over' is not necessarily positive. Reclaiming that knowledge may be difficult and may involve putting together again a fractured identity. That piece of 'personal experience' is no longer totally personal but has become in an irretrievable way the property of others. A dilemma of the Women's Studies classroom is that not all students are ready to take this step, do not understand its implications and as a result find the classroom an alienating situation.

This aspect of using experience in a Feminist inspired curriculum raises a number of dilemmas for the classroom participants. Once more the nature of the listening climate established becomes crucial. The distress that can result for participants is a dilemma that needs to be acknowledged and managed. Carol Gilligan (1982) has claimed that women's constructions of the moral domain focus on concepts of responsibility and caring. If this is the case, then a number of moral issues as well as those grounded in epistemic responsibility have to be juggled. Critical evaluation of another's experiential knowledge requires a degree of detachment. It places a heavy responsibility on the receivers of the personal disclosures, to return to the words of my student. That knowledge needs to be received with empathy but has to be evaluated with detachment. Moving between these modes of responding to the task of generating women's knowledge require skills of personal interaction and intellectual critical awareness which are awesome.

The preceding discussion of epistemological and pedagogic issues underpinning the Women's Studies curriculum has drawn attention to inseparable links between curriculum construction with its grounding in specific epistemological theory and pedagogic practice. The foregrounding of women's experience in the design and delivery of the Women's Studies curriculum necessitates both an appropriate epistemological construction in the context of the academy and the adoption of a Feminist inspired praxis. The resulting pedagogy presents practitioners both as learners and teachers with challenges and very great potential rewards.

3 Changing identities: two years on with Women's Studies

Mairead Owen

The title to this book is particularly apt. The contributors have been vividly aware of the ways in which Women's Studies does indeed act as a melting pot, for student, academics, readers and writers, listeners and speakers. It has certainly summed up the central theme of the research which is the subject of this chapter.

I teach at the Liverpool John Moores University where four years ago it was decided to initiate a BA Honours degree in Women's Studies. Since the degree was started we have all been subjected to the usual jokes, questions, battles, patronising attitudes, with which all lecturers and students of Women's Studies are familiar. Echoing bel hooks' (hooks, 1996, p.815) citing of 'the overall mainstream mocking of both Feminist thought and women's studies, which is one way the conservative backlash is attacking the work we do', we found while the objectivity of male knowledge was defended, feminist knowledge stood accused of being biased, subjective and political.

> Despite our hopes for the development of an oppositional culture, Women's Studies can become a cheap and cheerful addition to an institution's portfolio subsidised by women's political commitment ... responses can be characterised as ones of vague amusement, mixed with condescension occasioned by ignorance as to what Women's Studies is really about (Owen and Price, 1996, pp.168-169).

In studying Women's Studies, students are making a very active commitment. In the light of all the baggage which seems to accompany teaching and learning Women's Studies, I began to wonder who studies Women's Studies - and why?

I wanted to find out more about our students, their hopes, beliefs, attitudes, ambitions, so I decided to follow a cohort of Women's Studies students through their career with us. I used questionnaires as a basis, but the main method was in-depth interviews (conducted by a researcher who does not teach the students).

We interviewed the students as soon as they came to the University. The idea here was to interview them before they had become 'University students', trying to locate why indeed they had chosen Women's Studies, who they were, (demographic details) what were their hopes and fears, what were their family's attitudes to their studies. We started this with the intake of 1994 (our degree began in 1992 so this was the third intake) issuing questionnaires and conducting interviews immediately. We have already published and given conference papers about our findings about the students as they started their University careers (Owen, 1991, Owen and Price, 1996).

Now the students have completed their second year and are about to embark on their third and final year. I issued questionnaires last January/February and the interviews started in May and continued over the summer. I intend to issue the final questionnaires in May next year and hope to retain contact so that I can interview at least a proportion of the students one year after they graduate. The questionnaires are very open and lightly structured and we do in fact find that the questionnaires elicit almost written mini-interviews though obviously the in-depth interviews which are open-ended and can go on for a couple of hours develop a greater insight. (This is very much helped by the rapport which our interviewer has developed with the interviewees). We feel that the final interviews will be very useful with the respondents being able to put their whole experience of the degree into context.

In the context of this chapter there is not the space to give more than a brief description of the research method. However, we endeavoured to follow Feminist methodology as closely as possible (Bowles and Klein, 1983; Fonow and Cook, 1991; Stanley and Wise, 1992).

As I studied the responses to the questionnaire and what the students had said in their in-depth interviews it seemed to me that students were exceptionally aware, as they looked back to the time when they had come to the University, of the fact that they *had* changed (though there was one student who felt the degree had not changed her, yet went on to detail many ways in which changes had occurred). One observed wryly,

> It (the Women's Studies degree) should come with a government health warning. . . . Not everyone would want their cosy worlds turned upside down' (Transcript 19).

Another felt, 'I must have walked around blindfolded for years.'

This particular student 'never realised that I had been doing a 90 hour week with nothing to show at the end of it, no pay, no end product. When I read that Ann Oakley I sat at the table and sobbed.'

It seemed to me as I read the questionnaires and the transcripts of in-depth interviews that the changes fell into four areas though sometimes these overlapped.

1. Cognitive changes - the expansion of the 'world-taken-for-granted' to use the phenomenological expression, because of the acquiring of information.
2. Changes in practical self-image - ideas about physical appearance and ideas about psychological make-up.
3. Changes in relationships.
4. Changes in the apprehension of self-identity.

Though these are very rough and ready divisions and there is much overlap and blurring at the edges, I did find the divisions helped to order the information coming from the students.

Cognitive changes

Our basic trade is facts and figures, actual information. Sometimes in the Social Sciences (in which our Women's Studies degree is based) we are so aware of the situated nature of 'facts', of the disputed nature of the epistemologies with which we deal, that we can tend to underestimate the useful nature of the actual information to be found within the institution. Many students discovered, perhaps especially those who had been away from mainstream education for a while, though not these alone, that the expansion of their information base in itself was empowering. After all, in theory, one can sit in the library and access any information one needs. But more than this was the practice of gathering information, of marshalling that information into a reasoned debate, of learning to present an argument, of accepting critiques of that argument and going on to a new proposition, the old game of thesis, antithesis and of synthesis. One student remarked to me that before starting her degree she had looked at the broadsheet newspapers as almost written in a different dialect, certainly dealing with topics and arguments quite alien to her own life. Now they are an important source and 'they speak my language'. Very often information is directly and immediately useful as perhaps with Equal Opportunities issues. Worlds expand with information. 'Like I was saying about the third world politics, it's just stuff I never imagined . . . '

This student described how her learning 'had pushed her to do things' that she did not do at home. She had made new friends, joined the gym and now writes for the student magazine.

Another had phoned a work agency and had been fobbed off when she said she had not worked for quite a few years as she had been a full-time wife and then had gone to College. She had realised immediately afterwards that she should have approached the agency more systematically, listing the actual skills she had acquired, instead of the defensive and apologetic attitude she had adopted. She compared the desirable process to that of writing an assignment.

Self-Image Changes

A particular change was, to me, unexpected. Women's ideas about their own person, physical and psychological, seemed to undergo alteration. An obvious area was 'the fat is a feminist issue' arena. I am certainly not claiming that mere discussion of the social structuring around norms of the acceptable body is enough to cure deep psychological trauma. However, some students have said that they are moving towards a feeling that their bodies are their own and while not able to escape the cultural norm that thinner is healthier as well as more acceptable have begun to feel that it is a healthy body rather than a beautiful body they are after. Whether this is just a more acceptable definition in the competing discourses of femininity and of feminism, is difficult to say. Similarly, many students commented on their growing feeling that criticisms of what they think, or are interested in, or want to talk about, are irrelevant and they have a right to be themselves (of course whatever that might be) Students talked of the rejection of previously accepted roles: 'With age I'm getting a lot more bolshie!' (Transcript 1) Another said that she felt she had not changed in her feelings about her roles but 'Now I've got the academic background. I can back up what I've always thought and felt.' 'I can hold my own in a conversation and get other people to see my point of view.' (Transcript 16) 'I feel as though I can think for myself now ... I trust myself I suppose' (Transcript 19).

Relationships

Here there were very striking changes: between partners, with parents, with siblings, with children, with friends. I suppose the classic is the partner who cannot take the changes in the student. Sometimes this was an unwanted change which brought sadness. (In this part of the chapter I am concentrating on changes which have been seen by the students as empowering. I will look later at the 'downsides'. But in this instance the student saw the defection of the partner as a good thing.)

> *Researcher*: You said last time that he didn't help you very much and that you thought that would decline as the degree went on.

(The wording here is a little ambiguous but it seems from the context that both the researcher and the student had felt that the partner gave very little help and that even this would get less as the degree went on.)

> *Student*: Yes, yes, well that's how it's been. I mean he left just the week I was enrolling for my second year, and I thought "thanks very much". You know, no warning . . . So I thought I could do without somebody setting me up to fail like that all the time. I don't think that it was deliberate, but

whenever there's been a trauma it's been whenever I've had my exams or at the beginning of the academic year when you want to start fresh and get yourself organised and get yourself in a good habit, don't you, for the rest of the year.

The student did see the degree as playing a big part in the split up:

> I don't think he liked all the things that I found out and learnt and the things that dawned on me. I think men feel really threatened, don't they? I don't think people outside often realise the value of what the WS degree teaches or helps you to find out if you like. He sounded liberal when he talked but he didn't live that, he liked things to be traditional, ideology and all that (19).

One student had many problems, is attending a psychiatrist and has begun to feel that her problems stem from her relationship with her partner :

> He is jealous, possessive and very controlling. I don't want this and I'm trying to work at the relationship with my partner. He can't see (or doesn't want to see what he is doing). I think we are at a make or break point.

Others had managed to re-work their relationship: 'I'd like to educate men, their ignorance is sad'. This student appears to have done just this and notes the changes in her partner towards herself, his daughter and their nieces and nephews. This particular partner seems to have done a Women's Studies degree by proxy as the student tells how he reads her essays, hand-outs and books. The student believes they have a good relationship where they have shared the changes. Others had found new partners, 'He is at University himself . . . he is supportive over my doing the degree.' One student had married more or less as both she and her husband started University and felt that 'If the relationship has changed at all it has changed for the better, it has strengthened the relationship.' (Transcript 24) Women partners were generally perceived to be supportive and lesbian partnerships were seen as very positive though these were a minority in the respondents. Partners tended to be supportive even if not well versed in the argument:

> I know M (partner) isn't that interested but she's not interested in books or nothing like that but if I come home and tell her about the gay stuff or the lesbian stuff she's really interested. I expect support from her all the time (Transcript 11).

Relationships with other family members too were perceived to have changed. Those with mothers were a particular focus. A recurring theme among the student responses was that they often felt that their relationship with their mothers had improved in that through their studies they had developed an understanding of the difficult role of mothers and wives and the fact that in previous years these had been so constricting brought a new empathy.

One student described how her relationship with her mother in the past was 'terrible':

> This has come up in the course for me ... I realise now the difficulties of my mother's generation and how difficult it was for her. I'm kinder to her now and my mother is different to me now (student was implying a positive way) (Transcript 13).

A younger student felt: 'My relationship with my parents has changed, partially due to Women's Studies and partially just with going to University. I talk to my mum about feminist issues more.' (Transcript 18) In regard to children in general, for good or ill there seemed a definite movement to withdraw from an enveloping mothering role especially where older children were concerned and in fact this step had sometimes led to difficulties in the relationship. One respondent explained how she realised that it was not her responsibility to be a carer to her grown up son and this had caused 'havoc' and 'severe problems' for him and he has responded very aggressively.

In regard to daughters, usually a new empathy had grown up between respondents and daughters and indeed they seemed actively to be passing on what they were learning to their daughters. 'Women's Studies has affected my relationship with my daughter. I know I would have hemmed her in, but because of Women's Studies I'm different with her. I'm trying to let her be herself. She looks at things critically now, she's learned things through me. It's definitely because of Women's Studies.' One student said in relation to her small daughters, 'I've got three little femmies (sic) at home now.'

Difficulties were often reported in regard to friends. Respondents were aware of the changes they were undergoing as they gained experience in their degree work and I don't think there was one exception to the fact that students tended to compartmentalise friends. One student described it graphically: 'I have my friends from when I was at work, my "antenatal friends" and my friends from University.'

Identity

This, of course, is the crucial question. And it begets the whole enormous enterprise of the social sciences and the humanities at the moment, the question of identity and the self and what constitutes the 'subject' and what do we mean by changes in identity.

Before I embark on the changes in identity felt by the students I would just like to point to some of the possibly deleterious effects reported. I would not like to paint a picture of a Women's Studies degree as the panacea for all problems!

In some of the areas I have discussed students sometimes reported difficulties. In regard to the cognitive changes, there were the obvious difficulties of the influx of too much information, not enough time to assimilate this. There was also the factor of losing 'the innocent eye'. One student who took media courses complained that she could not enjoy television any more. She had become far too analytical and could not get inside the story. Coronation Street would never be the same again!

In regard to relationship changes, again it is obvious that these can be stressful. I have mentioned the compartmentalisation in regard to friends. This often led to a real sense of loss. One student returned to this theme several times. She now does not want to go to H(where her friend lives) because she 'feels so different now. At one time I used to love going there.' She talked nostalgically about this friend for a while in the interview. (Transcript 25) 'Friends. There have been changes. I've lost all my friends outside of the University. We're not as close.'

This respondent felt that in the first year of her Women's Studies she had become very 'opinionated' and had been 'totally emancipated from the humdrum life I lived.' A familiar desire was to shout it from the rooftops. Apparently she feels now that she might have been an embarrassment! She finds that what she and her friends had in common is drifting away and in fact she has more male friends now she reports.

One student was a lesbian and she raised some practical and some deeper questions. She would have liked far more courses devoted completely to lesbian issues. At the moment we do not run any modules specifically and completely on these though there are some gay and lesbian modules in other routes. We do, I hope, interweave lesbian issues as part of *all* our courses.

One of her points hit much more deeply:

> But some of the tutors who are teaching, they go home and they have a different view, they don't practise what they preach . . . I think you're telling me this but you're going home and doing something else. They tell you what you should be doing or what the ideal is, but it's not really like that, is it?

And again she commented about how people on the course would: 'say things like "everyone thinks you're a dyke because you are doing it (Women's Studies)". I'm thinking "well so what". I mean someone said that to me and I was like, "oh, yeah," really sarcastic'.

Weaving a thread through all the questionnaire responses and the transcripts of the interviews the question of identity seems the most crucial and in fact subsumes all others. This was the issue which emerged from the first questionnaires and interviews. Questions of the self and of identity are themselves in flux in present-day debate. There is an overwhelming focus on uncertainty, the shifting nature of the self, the impossibility of an integrity of identity. When the students reflected on their aims and interests, the search for a coherent self was a major enterprise. And now, two years on, students are considering their 'self' but also the changes in that self.

Certainly our students when asked to reflect on their experiences of their time with us, had a clear idea of a self identity albeit one which was fluid, changing, almost there to be discovered so that their own reactions came as a surprise sometimes.

> Yes, before I came back to education, the Access course, I was just a mum, just S's (child's) mum at school and you do get tied into that and lose your individuality and become S's mum and I feel that I've managed to shake that off a bit. Not all the time, you drift back into it when you're not at College or working.

Nevertheless, the students themselves, while using womanness as a frame, shift their position as cross-cutting aspects of their identity assume a greater significance. As the quotes from Transcript 11 showed, aspects like sexual orientation can assume a greater salience and indeed deny commonality:

> I have met loads of dead nice people doing this course who are people like me, even though they are not gay, they know that I am, they've got gay friends, whatever, and they're dead sound about it. But some, I don't know where these people come from, I don't know how you let them do a Women's Studies degree, they're just from a different planet to me. I don't know. (Do you not think that they are the people who need it more?) They just don't seem to take any notice. You tell them this stuff and whatever, and it just goes in one ear and out the other because they still have the same attitude towards it.

> I felt like a total nutter with the post-natal depression until I met someone in the coffee bar who had been through it.

As I have tried to show Women's Studies is, by no means, the answer to all women's problems and the research has indicated many points in our own practice which I want to change, develop, vary. Nevertheless it seems a crucial piece of the identity project. The research has made us very sensitive to our pedagogical practices, the theme of this book. We have realised that the degree is important to students and we must be careful in everything we do and say. Many of the changes that we have noted might well be the product of studying any University degree. Nevertheless I find myself amused when one student explained her reaction to learning about the inequalities of a patriarchal society: 'I get so angry, I get so annoyed about it. I feel like standing on a rooftop and shouting "do you realise?"'(Transcript 19).

And more soberly, a last quote which I think is a satisfying summing up of the value of studying Women's Studies and the changes which it brings:

Gaining confidence as a woman and as a person rather than somebody's appendage or somebody's mother. It's not a technical degree, it's not a vocational thing, it's about undoing all the damage that conventional education has done so far. That's what it's been like for me anyway, and having a bit more hope, not having such low expectations which I have been guilty of I think for the whole of my life (Transcript 19).

Note

Thanks to Karen Corteen, our talented and involved Researcher. Thanks also to all the students who took part, and continue to take part, in the research, for their thoughtful and considered input.

4 'The gift of intelligent rage'

Sue Graves

My name is Susan Graves, I am a part-time student at Edge Hill doing a BA Joint Honours degree in Applied Social Science and Women's Studies. I have three children and a full-time job as a lecturer at Skelmersdale College teaching administration courses mainly to women hoping to return to work after a break to bring up children.

Before I started the first year module I did not know what Women's Studies was and I was bowled over by what I learned. I had my consciousness well and truly raised. I realised that issues in my life which I perceived as personal failures were part of a wider structure of inequality. I recognised that rather than never having made the grade, I had never even been considered in the race - that the personal really was political.

I was so interested I read with gusto everything I could get my hands on. I discovered Betty Friedan (1993) and Ann Oakley (1974) writing about housework and motherhood and saying things that I instantly identified with. Germaine Greer (1970) and Gloria Steinem (1983, 1994) writing radical things about how women are stereotyped and steered into a narrow gender role and Sheila Rowbotham (1977a) and Gerda Lerner (1986) writing about how women are hidden from history, their experiences ignored and patriarchy perpetuated. Virginia Woolf (1928) writing about how the lack of a 'room of one's own' hinders personal academic success for women definitely hit a chord with me as did Charlotte Perkins Gilman (in Hayden, 1981) writing about how the design of homes and women's lack of personal space in them confines and constricts us. I was also fascinated to read of the work of Linda McDowell and Doreen Massey (1984) and their views of a Feminist geography particularly around the issue of gender and the organisation of space. The Matrix Group (1984) of women architects have fascinating things to say about how inequality is endemic in the built environment and how this perpetuates gender roles in society. Charlotte Perkins Gilman (1966 ed.) also got me interested in economics which I viewed in a completely different light once I had read Gloria Steinem's (1994) deconstruction of the ways in which the GNP and GDP are calculated. I was in awe at the power of language once I had read Dale Spender's *Man Made Language* (1990) and the work of Deborah Tannen (1994) about the use of language and how women's self effacing and conciliatory style disadvantages them at work and perpetuates the status quo. I read Susie Orbach's (1978) groundbreaking views on how women's obsession with weight and dieting should be viewed as a Feminist issue as she feels this is an expression of women's alienation from their own bodies as a result of living as second class citizens in society. Also fascinating is Kim Chernin's (1983) more radical assertion that the tyranny of slenderness is an aspect of male violence against women which supports the patriarchy which denies all women the right to grow and look mature.

I was all over the library looking at Feminism from different angles and revelling in what I was discovering. My interest meant I was covering a diverse range of subject areas - Geography, History, Psychology, English, Architecture and the Built Environment - which I would never have touched on if I had not been doing Women's Studies.

This was the honeymoon phase. In year two I felt curiously flat and depressed. How did my newfound insights into women's subordination affect my life? It did not - I had changed my perceptions of almost everything but my life was exactly the same, same job, same family, same me.

Now I was a Feminist what should I do differently - what could I do that I had not done before - what does a Feminist do? How can I change things, my reading had shown me that the issues were embedded everywhere - I felt as though I had had a protective skin removed and I was vulnerable. My everyday world seemed to be filled with examples of women's inferior status in society which drove me mad, television adverts, soap operas, newspaper articles, comments from colleagues at work, expectations of children and husband at home. I was like a women possessed feeling I was constantly at odds with the world, complaining about everything and everyone.

I was accused more than once of being a raving Feminist loony, the scales had fallen from my eyes and it was painful to look at the world anew and realise how my place in it was determined to such an extent by my biology. I felt powerless to determine my own, or my daughter's destiny and I was angry. It was a time of looking back on my life, my childhood, adolescence, teenage years and so on and discovering how I had been socialised to expect less from myself and from others, and always to give more than I felt I was entitled to receive.

This is how it felt being a mature Women's Studies student - it can mean a painful re-evaluation of a life and it can make you unhappy and resentful of past iniquities. Being a part-time student who only came in for scheduled lectures and seminars I missed the informal support of the group, I would have really liked to be part of a women's group to meet and discuss issues. I searched in vain for a women's magazine which debated the issues I was interested in but to no avail. Luckily my sister had taken some Women's Studies classes and she provided a well-informed ear as did my female colleagues at work who continue to be a source of guidance, inspiration and support.

My newfound insights made me look at things differently, for example my daughter's primary school has two large playgrounds and I noticed that both were taken over by boys playing football and the girls clustered in groups around the edge with no space to run and play and have some space and freedom. This had always been the case and I have had three children at this school, the other two boys, but I had never considered the implications of this takeover of public space by boys before. So I mentioned my concern to the female head teacher and suggested that only one playground be allocated for football and the other be left free for everyone else. She was very interested in my opinion and did in fact put this rule in place.

I felt good, a practical application of what I had been reading about gender and public space, maybe it would make a difference to all the little girls who now had opportunity to run and play uninhibited. My daughter, however, was mortified that I had been instrumental in this and banned me from picking her up from school, insisting she was old enough to walk home with her friends. Doing Women's Studies has meant that our Mother/Daughter disputes about shoes, clothes, hair etc are tinged with my Feminist ideas about how girls' identities are shaped and bound up with these issues. For example, our predictable arguments about what constitutes 'sensible' school shoes are over-shadowed by my desire for her not to be constrained by heels or over-fussy designs, for her to have freedom of movement to walk and run through her world with the ease which boys do. Her choice of clothes, especially in this era of short skirts and overtly 'feminine' styles is dampened by my desire for her not to put herself in this category. I am keen for her to do a lot of sport and to see herself as strong and fit - for her growing awareness of her body to be a positive experience. I am trying to steer her away from an emphasis on the physical appearance that is synonymous with this age group (she is 11). I want her to be confident to express her opinions and not take a 'back seat' - sometimes to be angry without feeling it is 'unfeminine'. She on the other hand wants to be the same as her friends and 'fit in' - she has to live in the world as it is - having a mother who takes issue with the most mundane aspects of your life must be wearying for her. So we compromise, I tell her my objections, she listens and we try to steer a middle course - I am hopeful that the things I try to impart to her now which she cannot always understand, will hold her in good stead for the future.

Feminism in practice is not easy for me or those I come into contact with. Using what I have learned in my everyday life means that my teenage sons cannot get away with casual sexist remarks or actions, life at home has been transformed along anti-sexist living lines (a la Jo Van Every) which means we start from a point of two adults sharing a house, both with full time jobs and then sharing this other job called housework and parenting - sharing the work and the responsibility.

At work it means valuing my female colleagues and taking a conscious decision to ask them for help or advice, especially technical advice, rather than male colleagues. It means re-thinking my everyday transactions for example as a Feminist how do I defend paying the person who services my car (invariably male) a higher hourly rate than the person who looks after my children (invariably female) - I get round this by using a female car mechanic (when I can, they are incredibly hard to find) but am aware this does not tackle the issue of work which is seen as a 'female' being undervalued. I have made a point of using a female plumber and always ask for a female driver if I need a cab - it is not always as quick to arrange, but I figure it is the least I can do to support these women who must find it hard working in male dominated areas. It also has the advantage of giving my children experience of women doing diverse things.

All this of course marks me out and makes me the butt of numerous Feminist taunts and accusations of political correctness, it would be easier to deny I am a Feminist rather than to proclaim it readily as I do - but I feel that being a Feminist is one of the most positive things in my life. I feel it is an admirable thing to be a Feminist and stand up for one's own sex, to fight against inequality and injustice - even in the small ways I have described.

This year as part of my studies I undertook some research into transport policy and how it impacts on the lives of women living in Skelmersdale New Town. I used my own students at Skelmersdale College for this research and chose this topic because from experience I knew how lack of convenient, affordable transport constrains their lives. I identified with this as I recognised that my own experiences of owing a car had enabled me to maintain a measure of independence even through the child rearing years that was denied to these women.

They were extremely eager to talk to me and revelled in the experience of having their concerns listened to and taken seriously. Their sense of self-worth was definitely enhanced by the opportunity to be valued and by having someone so interested in them. I realised what a powerful thing it is to take people's stories and put them 'out there' - what was I going to do with all these heartfelt testimonies? Surely the point of doing Feminist research was to improve the lot of women? Anyway how was my research Feminist? It was not just Feminist because I was doing it surely? What was I doing differently than any 'non Feminist researcher'? Was I using them to enhance myself? They unburdened to me because they thought I was in a position of power to do something to improve things for them. I did not see myself as a researcher, I did not feel confident with that label.

I moved between the position of awareness of similarities between this group and myself, ie children, problems of working, studying and housework - we had similar knowledge to trade - to an awareness of acute differences. Did my position as their tutor mean I was exploiting them? Perhaps they felt they could not refuse to allow me into their lives? They all knew where I was coming from, I made no secret of my Feminist ideas, was I influencing them in a hierarchical way? For a lot of them it was the first time anyone had taken such an interest in them and their lives - there were a lot of disclosures of a personal nature during these interviews.

For example, when talking about their reluctance to go out at night, even by car, I was ready with the official statistics which I thought would convince them of the extremely small likelihood of their being attacked - after all I had done 'fear of Crime' in my criminology module and had read how women's fear of crime was out of all proportion with the actuality. I was eager to tell them this, for them to reclaim the night and be empowered by this knowledge. How wrong I was, from the 15 women I talked to, two had in fact been physically attacked, one seriously sexually assaulted and another had been subjected to a protracted campaign of obscene telephone calls from a neighbour. Only the last of these incidents had been reported to the police so they did not show on any official statistics.

Besides that, they reminded me that when they were out at night encountering groups of men held the terror of not knowing what would happen - the uncertainty of whether the mild catcalls and jibes of a group of teenage boys would escalate into something more was extremely frightening and it was this that kept them at home. I was chastened and reminded of Gloria Steinem's (1994) advice to use personal experience to challenge theory.

I read Liz Kelly's (1988) work on the subject of male violence and felt that her theory of a continuum - with catcalls at one end and serious assault and murder at the other - gave more of an idea of what women experienced. I realised I had been looking at this from a male perspective and just accepted what all the male commentators told me women's experiences were. The realities for females are very different from the picture that was presented to me at my criminology lecture - women's fear of male violence is well founded and has a controlling effect on us all.

Again this brings up implications at a personal level, I let my teenage sons experience a level of freedom that I know I will find difficult to extend to my daughter when the time comes. On the one hand I know what the implications of this lack of freedom of movement may have on her, but on the other as a mother I feel an overwhelming desire to keep her safe and do feel that the world is less safe for her - what do I do? What choice will do the least damage? Not for me the easy route of my less enlightened friends who feel no discomfort in insisting on tight boundaries for their daughters that they do not impose on their sons. As I said, being a Feminist is not easy - it means re-thinking almost every area of your life.

At the end of the day with my students at Skelmersdale I think I overestimated my influence with them. I watched as they weighed up my Feminist explanations against their own beliefs and experience, evaluated its usefulness for their lives and discarded what they did not want. They realised more than I did that what they really needed was access to money, power and authority to change the structure and inequalities which make up their lives.

I intend to continue my research and am reading everything I can about doing research from a Feminist perspective. I am also keeping a diary of my experiences and feelings which I feel will be useful in showing the process of the research.

What I feel doing Women's Studies has given me is - in the words of Patricia Williams (1991) - 'the gift of intelligent rage'. I realise I have always had the rage, but doing Women's Studies has given me insights into what my rage is about, it has helped me to ask the questions - and answered a few. I intend to finish my degree - I graduate in 1999 - and have already decided I would like to do post graduate work in the area of Women's Studies. In the meantime, I take heart from the words of John Stuart Mill written in 1869 (Stibbs, 1983):

> The most important thing women have to do is to stir up the zeal of women themselves.

- and I promise to keep stirring things up!

5 What can tutors and students do to promote egalitarian relationships in the Women's Studies classroom?

Penny Welch

Introduction

> Feminist education - the feminist classroom - is and should be a place where there is a sense of struggle, where there is visible acknowledgement of the union of theory and practice, where we work together as teachers and students to overcome the estrangement and alienation that have become so much the norm in the contemporary university (hooks,1989, p.51).

I am still as excited and inspired by this quotation as I was when I first read it five years ago. It tells me that teaching is a worthwhile activity, that reflecting on teaching and learning is a valid form of scholarship, that my professional practice can, and should be, congruent with my political beliefs and that students and teachers can work together for positive personal and social change.

The political, intellectual and material conditions within which teachers attempt to 'make a difference' change over time and vary considerably between different countries, different sectors of the educational system and different institutions within the same sector. I do not want to start this chapter by making any predictions about what will be the central concerns of committed teachers, including those who identify themselves as feminist teachers, in five or ten years time. However, against the background of the global information revolution and the emphasis by governments on post school education as a key factor in economic growth and development, the expansion of interest in issues of teaching and learning that can be observed in the 1990s, looks set to continue into the next century.

Feminist pedagogy

The ideas and arguments put forward in this piece are based on a fairly consistent attempt over a number of years to reflect on my own practice as a teacher of Women's Studies and Politics in a new university (ex-polytechnic) located in an industrial town in the English Midlands. My reflection is informed by dialogue with students and colleagues and by reading a small selection of the extensive international literature on progressive pedagogy, on innovation in teaching and learning methods and on Women's Studies in an academic setting. My aim in writing is not to exhort the reader to adopt any or all of my particular perspectives or practices, except that of being a reflective practitioner. This chapter follows on from my initial attempt to construct systematically a way of teaching and relating to students with which I, as a white, forty-something, anti-racist feminist and socialist could be comfortable. In that piece I identified three principles that could form a basis for a feminist pedagogy that I saw as most realisable in Women's Studies but with potential for application in other subjects. These three principles are:

1. To strive for egalitarian relationships in the classroom.
2. To try to make all students feel valued as individuals.
3. To use the experience of students as a learning resource (Welch,1994).

In arriving at these three principles, I was indebted to many colleagues and students who discussed their classroom experiences with me, to the early writers on Women's Studies in Britain (Edney and Langton, 1974; Bird, 1980) as well as the later ones (Evans,1982; Currie and Kazi,1987; Aaron and Walby, 1991), and to a variety of authors whose educational philosophies are grounded in the practicalities of teaching (hooks,1989; Freire,1972; Rogers,1951).

Two years on, despite coming across additional problems with the concept of Feminist pedagogy (Gore,1993) and being much less convinced that I could make the classroom a safe place to share distressing personal experiences (Luke,1994), I feel fairly confident that I, and others who have arrived at similar conclusions, can find many ways of implementing the second and third principles outlined above. Remembering names, saying hello on campus, keeping regular consultation hours, really listening when students raise personal or academic concerns, remembering students' previous work, making it clear that one is judging the assignment and not the student, returning work promptly with constructive comments, are all ways of showing students they are valued as individuals. Using the experience of students as a learning resource can be widely interpreted and might include their experience of racism, imperialism or xenophobia, of sexism, poverty or homophobia, their involvement in political campaigns, their work experiences and their experience of studying. Barbara Omolade (1993, p.34) summarises one way in which the experiential and the academic can be integrated:

When I am teaching history and politics, my students can bring their experience, insights and questions to classroom discussions. I assist them by adding the factual, analytical and contextual information that illuminates and expands their insights. The method works well to empower students, drawing them out, helping them to make sense of what they already know and have experienced.

Problems with power

However I do feel much less secure in my ability to encourage egalitarian relationships in the classroom and in the next five subsections I want to explore what for me are key concerns.

Why do I want to promote egalitarian relationships?

Central to the philosophy that inspired early attempts to take Feminism into the academy in the form of Women's Studies and to several theories of pedagogy that I find attractive is the advocacy of making the tutor-student relationship as equal as possible. These include the co-operative problem -posing model of education (Freire,1972); the student-centred method of teaching (Rogers,1951), liberatory pedagogy (hooks,1989), and the student empowerment approach (Shrewsbury,1993). Freire sees his method as appropriate only to educational projects outside the formal system of education in an exploitative society but the other three explain how their approaches can make learning more effective within institutions of Higher Education in a country like the USA. Rogers argues that unequal relationships inhibit learning because they tend to make people uncomfortable or threatened. bell hooks believes that not just the content of classes but the teaching methods used must challenge domination and oppression. Caroline Shrewsbury advocates tutor-student interaction that builds up the skills and confidence of the students. Higher Education teachers who feel positive about these ideas and who wish to make their classrooms places where the power differentials between tutor and students are reduced could start by considering what aspects of their courses might be open to negotiation with students and within what parameters. Aspects of the course not up for negotiation can also be discussed with students and the reasoning behind decisions already made can be explained. Teaching methods that maximise active participation by students in the classroom (small group work and whole class discussion, inviting both affective and cognitive responses to the topic, integrating academic and experiential knowledge), assessment tasks that encourage independent thought and action by students (individual and group projects, negotiated essay titles, oral and visual presentations, assessment of skills as well as knowledge), openness and transparency in the assessment process (clear, published assessment criteria, negotiation of deadlines, rapid feedback, elements of self-assessment) and formal or informal systems of student feedback about the course can be important elements in an egalitarian approach to teaching and can be introduced gradually, evaluated and if necessary amended.

How genuinely egalitarian can I be?

If openness and negotiation are important characteristics of an egalitarian approach, pretence is clearly counter-productive. I believe that it is very important not to ignore the different roles and responsibilities that tutors and students have. or to dismiss the very real power imbalances that exist. For example, I am given status, authority and a salary by the university for which I work. I am given the ability to contribute to the design of courses, schemes of assessment and the rules that govern the grading of formal qualifications. Within these arrangements, I have the power to assess the work of students and I may be asked to write confidential references, not only on their academic performance, but on their character and personality. Notwithstanding the current emphasis on student charters and students as customers (Skeggs,1995), students have only limited countervailing rights of complaint and representation and some opportunity to evaluate my work through end of module questionnaires. My standard of living is higher than the majority of students that I teach, my life as a student nearly thirty years ago was a lot easier, materially and emotionally, than theirs is now. I brought to my undergraduate study more cultural capital than today's working class or lower middle class mature students who left school at 15 or 16 do and I do not face racism, homophobia or discrimination as do Black students, lesbian and gay students and students with disabilities. Where I share a similar standard of living with some of my students and perhaps live in the same neighbourhood or belong to the same community groups, the power differential is reduced a little. The unequal power relationship between the students and me seems to have two dimensions at least. I have greater social power within and outside the academy than they do and from time to time I am obliged to exercise power over them. However, within the boundaries of the law, institutional rules and academic custom and practice, I have the choice of emphasising and reinforcing that unequal power relationship or of minimising it. If I choose to minimise it because I am convinced that inequalities of power inhibit learning, it is still my choice and one that I can revoke. There is also some danger that I will convince myself that I am being egalitarian when I am only exercising my greater power in a different way.

In discussions about Women's Studies and about Feminist pedagogy, power over others is often distinguished from the power to do things for oneself . The first is referred to as domination (negative) and the second as empowerment (positive). Since I read a very incisive critique of the use of the word 'empower' as something a teacher could do to or for a student, I have realised that there is still a danger in that concept of casting the student in a passive role and one that probably remains subordinate. 'It is because someone, some agent, is to do the empowering, that the teacher's authority as the agent of that empowerment seems to be so troubling within the discourse of feminist pedagogy' (Gore,1993, p.74). Perhaps it would be better to avoid using the word 'empower' without spelling out clearly what is meant. 'The tutor can use her/his power and influence to create the conditions in which the student can more easily or more fully develop confidence and a sense of personal efficacy' is a formulation that appeals to me because it indicates the different roles and responsibilities of tutor and students.

Even though departing from the traditional role of the academic is difficult and complicated, I believe it is worthwhile to demonstrate to students, through openness, negotiation and respect, that one is giving up at least some of the opportunities available to exercise domination over them. The extent of the fear expressed by many students, that good grades are dependent on reproducing the ideas of the lecturer or that a lecturer might, if offended by criticism or complaint, award lower grades than the work deserves, appears to me to be much greater than the very occasional incident of such unprofessional behaviour would seem to warrant. I suspect that such a perspective is more a reflection of student awareness of the unequal power relationship that I outlined above, of their belief, fostered by a divided and unequal society and a hierarchical school system, that the lecturer's job is to deposit knowledge in the student (Freire,1972), and their direct experience of lecturers who are unapproachable or autocratic or just plain rude.

Are tutors always more powerful than students?

I must also allow for the fact that not all students behave impeccably to tutors or to each other. Well-established lecturers are faced from time to time by discourtesy, verbal harassment and frivolous complaints from students, which can be upsetting and energy consuming. It can be much more serious when tutors who are inexperienced or on temporary contracts, from an ethnic minority or another country, disliked by institutional management or otherwise vulnerable, have to deal with sneering comments, malicious complaints or a deliberately disruptive class. In those circumstances, tutors do not have, or do not believe they have, more power than students. They need support form union representatives and other colleagues to prevent themselves being victimised by managers and to help them stop the students behaving oppressively. I have not had enough experience of supporting colleagues in these circumstances to put forward specific suggestions that could help with this problem and I have not come across any relevant academic literature yet. NATFHE and AUT will clearly offer advice to members in individual cases and may also have published some guidance. I will turn later to the issue of students behaving oppressively to each other.

How can tutors make sure they treat all students equally?

The points I make in this section are applicable across all subjects in Higher Education. Impartial systems of assessment and for the consideration of circumstances that justify the late submission of work, sufficient library resources and access to information technology, the provision of all key information in written module guides that are distributed to all students, are only the start. Whatever the tutor's own social characteristics, it is worth practising the use of inclusive language (s/he, her/his etc), avoiding the metaphorical use of words like blind or Black to indicate something negative, not saying 'women' when what is really meant is white women or heterosexual women or Western women. Sensitivity to the feelings of students needs to be exercised particularly in the way the tutor receives each contribution in a class discussion s/he is facilitating. Students say that the most discouraging response they can get is for their contribution to be ignored. Any feelings the student might have about not being fully entitled to be in Higher Education are increased, particularly if the student comes from a group that is underrepresented in Higher Education and/or s/he faces discrimination in everyday life.

A further bad reaction that students can get is to be told that their view or answer is wrong. Perhaps there are a lot of tutors in Higher Education posing questions for class discussion that are capable of having right or wrong answers instead of those which are open to different perspectives and interpretations? Or perhaps critical responses by the tutor to what the students say are interpreted by some students as negating the whole value of their contribution. Some tutors and students do argue that some differentiation by the tutor between the most illuminating and the least illuminating student contributions is necessary as guidance to the learning of the rest of the student group. My perspective is that this underestimates the ability of students to distinguish that difference for themselves. Tutors who participate in workshops will know that a significant part of their learning occurs as they listen to how the various points made relate to one another and as they try to formulate their own contribution. I would certainly advocate that whatever the range of responses used by a tutor, s/he locates them at the positive end of the spectrum.

How far is it possible to encourage egalitarian relationships between students without exercising a degree of control or direction?

In this section I am going to talk specifically about Women's Studies classes. The way the question is posed reflects my preference for making the classroom as permissive and non-threatening as possible. This preference can probably be traced back to my socialisation as a student in the late 1960s. But it was not until the late 1980s, ironically in discussions held under the auspices of Enterprise in Higher Education (an initiative sponsored and funded by the Department of Employment in 1987 in order to inculcate business related skills and values in undergraduates), that I fully recognised that I could enter the classroom without assuming the artificial role of the 'expert' and without seeing the students as an audience I needed to impress or manipulate or control. I could stop thinking in terms of 'lectures' and 'seminars' and instead plan a range of classroom activities. I could focus on what and how students would learn in the classroom rather than on what and how I would teach. If I discovered from experience or from student feedback that certain activities did not facilitate student learning as well as planned, the activities could be changed, refined or dropped. As a result, I felt more comfortable and confident in the classroom. I was using a greater range of skills than in the traditional lecture or seminar but I felt under much less stress. The activities I planned for students were also intended to enhance their ability to speak, listen, develop lines of argument, solve problems and to deepen their understanding of the subject matter, without putting them under undue pressure. Small group work and whole class discussion turned out to be particularly useful and versatile activities. I later found theoretical justification for the overall approach I was using in Carl Rogers, who argues that the teacher (or facilitator) needs to *trust* the capacity of the students to think for themselves and to learn for themselves (Rogers, 1983, p.871).

I believe that trusting students to make what they feel is the best use of the learning opportunities in the classroom is an approach that enhances learning and so I do not oblige all students to speak, I do not lay down ground rules for the conduct of discussion and I am not disapproving of those who miss classes or leave early. One drawback of this approach is that I then have no way of attempting to ensure that all students get an equal amount out of the classes. My classes generally have a calm and co-operative atmosphere. Discussion may get heated but in the vast majority of exchanges there is no sign of personal animosity or attempts to devalue the contributions of others. Consequently I have not needed to develop a repertoire of interventions to deal with situations where conflict arising from inequalities or differences between students has made the classroom obviously uncomfortable. This does not mean, however, that some students are not feeling anxious or tense or angry. I do not know if the students who say very little are exercising a completely free choice or whether they are silenced by feelings of difference, inequality or inferiority - whether intellectual, ideological or social. Responses to a recent pilot questionnaire I distributed indicated that a minority of Level 2 (but not Level 3) students feel reluctant to express views that are different from those of the tutor or that might be unpopular with other students. I was pleased to note that neither Black students nor older students were over-represented in this small minority but I will need to find ways of discussing the issue identified. I will probably talk about it when I hand out the questionnaire again and say that I would welcome written points from students on how it might be dealt with. Kelly Coate Bignell argues for more writing about Feminist pedagogy that is informed by the perspectives of students themselves. Her own research confirmed that some of the Women's Studies students felt marginalised if they did not agree with the views expressed by the majority of the student group (Bignell,1996).

Feminist teachers have different responses to the question of intervention. The first three I cite all work in the USA. bell hooks believes strongly the Women's Studies classroom must be a challenging rather than a safe or comfortable place. Her aim is to 'encourage students to come to voice in an atmosphere where they may be afraid or see themselves at risk. The goal is to enable all students, not just an assertive few, to feel empowered in a rigorous, critical discussion' (hooks,1989, p.53). In pursuit of this aim she obliges all students to read aloud in class and makes attendance mandatory. A writer who is interventionist in a different way is Lynn Weber Cannon who teaches courses on 'race'. She lays down ground rules for classroom discussion at the beginning of the course which include students agreeing not to blame themselves for previous misinformation about their own group or other groups in society, not perpetuating such misinformation, not blaming 'victims' for the condition of their lives, never devaluing the experience of other people and agreeing to combat actively myths and stereotypes about their own and other groups (Cannon, 1990).

Nancy Schniedewind uses negotiation to reduce the differences of power between herself and the students and to reduce competition and conflict between students. Expectations of the course are shared, and within limits she sets, mutually agreed. Regular feedback sessions occur, with the instructor responding to anonymous written comments from the students. Students can decide in advance whether to do the assignments and reach the level required for an A, B or C. She also teaches students how to use 'I-messages' - statements about how the behaviour of a fellow student makes the student giving the message feel - and encourages them to use them. The example that she gives is 'Sue, when you dominate the class discussion, I feel annoyed because I'm interested in hearing the thoughts of everyone here.' (Schniedewind, 1983, p.263).

The least interventionist Feminist writers and teachers that I found were Louise Morley and Philomena Essed. Louise Morley teaches Women's Studies to students on a post-experience professional youth and community workers course in the UK. She gives examples of students becoming frustrated and angry with each other in discussions on 'race' and on sexuality. In the second example she states:

> I needed to provide a challenge to the heterosexism in the group without it being seen as authority-led and thereby activating more unhelpful feelings. But more importantly, I needed to share my thinking about group process and interrupt the destructive blaming games that were being enacted. (Morley, 1993, p.127).

Philomena Essed writes about interactions on the courses she runs on women and racism in the Netherlands. She attempts to make sure that structural conflict is discussed at a societal rather than at a personal level. She avoids, for example, criticising students directly for using racist terms that are in common use in the Netherlands, but rather incorporates explanations of why they are racist in the presentations she gives (Essed, 1994).

I have run a workshop with the same title as this chapter. I asked each group to make a collective list of what the tutors in the group had done to be more egalitarian with students and what the students in the group had done to be more egalitarian with other students. I then asked them to discuss occasions where inequalities between students had made the classroom uncomfortable. Both groups spent more time on the first task and in their reports back stressed negotiation, within ground rules established by tutors and reflecting institutional constraints, over assignments, assessment criteria and classroom activities. There was an emphasis on encouraging students to take responsibility for activities such as group work and to see the outcome of classes as a responsibility shared with tutors. The role of staff in establishing an atmosphere of mutual respect was highlighted and in response to the problem identified in the second task, it was agreed that tutors needed to have the courage to intervene when students were acting oppressively to each other. As facilitator, I got the impression that the participants in the workshop welcomed the opportunity to share ideas and experiences but that the discussion at the end lacked the spark it might have had if I had strongly advocated certain approaches to teaching and invited responses from the whole group.

That started me thinking about how organising classes or conference sessions around group work, shared tasks, and open-ended discussion questions may be in one sense very egalitarian but in another sense is not because the parameters of the interaction and discussion are set by the tutor or facilitator in advance. I dislike being in academic contexts where confrontation is positively invited although I have no problems with confrontational situations in staff meetings or in union-management meetings. But in always trying to set up a teaching/learning context that is as co-operative as possible, I may be denying students the opportunity to experience confrontation and challenge in a way that strengthens them all. My next task is to explore ways of providing that opportunity without losing what is positive in my current approach.

6 Women's Studies in Human Geography

David A. Halsall

This chapter is concerned with links between Women's Studies and Human Geography: why women's issues should be studied in Human Geography, why a Feminist Geography is of value, how staff and students respond to the challenges of these approaches, are associated and crucial issues. Possible answers to these problems reflect the varying approaches of Geography and of Women's Studies and the contemporary situation within the world as a whole. Concepts of 'space' and 'place' underpin much geographical thought, and given that women's lives and actions, take place in, are affected by, and affect, the nature of space and place, women's situations should have at least an equal analysis to those of men, in the portrayal of and search for understanding of these relationships. Moreover 'the academic discipline of Geography has historically been dominated by men, perhaps more so than any other human science' (Rose, 1993, p.1), and the relationships between gender, knowledge and power are apparent within its structures, ideas and approaches, and reflect albeit often unconsciously and unintentionally, 'that inequalities between the sexes have not been eradicated' (WGSG, 1984) whether in 'advanced' or 'developing' countries. The focus is herewith on *Human* Geography, deliberately so, because whilst the dichotomy of geographic scholastic endeavours between human and physical sides of the discipline do meet, as in studies of environmental problems, it is in Human Geography that links with other humanities and social sciences, and with Women's Studies can most readily be developed. There are issues in Physical Geography too to which a Feminist approach should be applied, but these are not developed here.

The persistence of the domination of Geography personnel by men is well documented (McDowell, 1979, 1990; Bondi and Peake, 1988, p.218, Knox, 1991, p.91). Nevertheless, during the last decade considerable progress has been achieved in Feminist research in British Geography departments. McDowell and Peake (1990, p.20) identify a series of trends and topics in the development of

Feminist Geography accompanied by key publications (Table 1). Topic 6 is represented by Bell and Valentine (1995).

Table 1
McDowell's and Peake's changing emphases in Feminist Geography (1990)

1	*'The spatial behaviour of women* (Tivers, 1978; McDowell, 1979; Foord, 1980)'
2	*'An analysis of the social relations between men and women* (Bowlby et al, 1982)'
3	*'Social and spatial structures that create and reinforce women's oppression* (MacKenzie and Rose, 1983; McDowell, 1983; Bowlby and McDowell, 1986)'
4	*'The definition of patriarchy* (Foord and Gregson, 1986; McDowell, 1986)'
5	*'Interrelationships between class, race and gender* (Fincher, 1989; Rose, 1989)'
6	*'Issues of subjectivity and sexuality as well as the economic basis of women's subordination'*

Furthermore, this development of Feminist Geography is accompanied by other core volumes which are recognised as key Human Geography texts in a recent (male writer's) chronology of the discipline (Rogers, 1996), and a new journal since 1994, *Gender, Place and Culture*. Bowlby's (1989) summary of progress in Feminist Geography in Britain is placed in a world wide context (Peake (ed), 1989) in which research in countries such as Brazil retains a strong androcentric focus (Calio, 1989) although there is increasing published work on gender and development studies (Momsen & Townsend, 1987; Momsen & Kinnaird, 1993). 'Despite ten or more years of published work on women, gender relations and Feminist approaches to geographical issues ... geographical teaching remains relatively untouched by feminism and by Feminist theoretical perspectives ... the curriculum of Human Geography is still overwhelmingly concerned with an ungendered subject'. (McDowell, 1992, pp.185-6) McDowell's report on ongoing discussions in the WGSG to rectify this situation suggests five areas of challenge (Table 2).

Table 2
WGSG challenges (McDowell, 1992)

1. *'Making space'*: what do geographers omit in existing curricula to make space for Feminist perspectives?
2. *'The problem of translation'*: of 'making Feminist discourse both intelligible and familiar to colleagues who have less knowledge of contemporary Feminist debates than others' especially given the great volume of Feminist literature outside Geography.
3. *'Questions of difference'*: the 'variety of experiences of women including views of different race, colour, culture'.
4. *'Classroom and fieldwork relations'*: the traditional male orientated socialisation in Geography and impact on equal opportunities.
5. Debates re the place of *'Women's Studies or Gender Studies'* and the relations of the latter with Feminist critical theory.
6. *'The (Im)possibility of Paradigm Shift'*: discussions re the nature of change and the existence of differing views and approaches, eg a number of different geographies rather than one holistic approach.

These problems and challenges to teaching as well as research are compounded by the unfamiliarity of many Geography students with gender issues unless these have been encountered in subjects other than Geography at school level. There is little recognition of gender/women's issues in GCSE or 'A' level Geography syllabuses, or in school text books, although the established 'A' level volume by Waugh (1996) now contains brief sections on gender, employment and development. In journals aimed at school teachers, critiques of sexism in Geography text books (Wright, 1985; Atkinson, 1992) and resources (Warner, 1993) are only recently complemented by discussions on curricular content in response to the National Curriculum (Connolly, 1993) and to trends in research in Feminist Geography in higher education (Townsend and Townsend, 1988; Bowlby, 1992). The geographical experiences at school level where generally gender is not identified as an issue results in a 'neutered' and 'neutralised' Geography as a context in which Year One undergraduates have been nurtured. The strategies of teaching gender and Feminist issues and approaches within a broad Human Geography foundation module and the challenges they place upon staff and students form the basis of much of this chapter.

Setting foundations for students' understanding of Feminist Geography

The introduction of gender issues and Feminist approaches to the first year Human Geography group at Edge Hill University College illustrates some of the experiences and challenges indicated above. The aims of the first year Human Geography module encompass four broad groups - geographical, intellectual, personal and technical. Of necessity gender and Feminist Geography is a small specific section with explicit relationships with further themes. It comprises two introductory sessions on Feminist approaches, sexist and non-sexist attitudes in Geography, and gender inequality in a patriarchal society. These are related to specific situations and activities in further sessions, especially on access and mobility, travel constraints and opportunities and transport provision (discussed below); employment and unemployment (developing from Massey, 1984) and gender relationships, place and communities (based upon McDowell's and Massey's geographical interpretations of historical scholarship, 1984).

Selected quantitative and qualitative methods and survey techniques are included in a practical component, and the use of non-sexist language (based upon publication guidelines in the journal *Area*) is further discussed in a tutorial situation. For assessment, students can choose a 1,500 word assignment, a fieldwork poster, and a structured examination question all of which could be based upon gender/women's issues.

The intended outcomes of this foundation work in Feminist Geography are that students should :

(i) Gain an experience of gender/women's issues, and of Feminist approaches, early in their undergraduate career so as to give a foundation of knowledge, understanding and thought;

(ii) Gain confidence to appreciate Feminist material in Part 2 of the degree; (Previously undergraduates had to wait until Year 3 for work in Feminist Geography and thus lacked the background for dissertations or other opportunities for individual or group work.)

(iii) Appreciate the value, at an introductory level, of a Feminist approach in constructing a balanced view of human interaction in space, and in the development of place;

(iv) Appreciate the role of gender relations within spatial aspects of society, again at an introductory level;

(v) Develop skills of writing in a non sexist style, sympathetic to women and men.

The overall intention too is to increase students' confidence in dealing with gender issues in Geography, to empower women students by demonstrating that women's lives matter in Human Geography as much as those of men, by increasing *all* the students' (women's and men's) gender awareness. This is perhaps a beginning towards McDowell's ideas of a transformed curriculum in Human Geography (1992).

Teaching ideas and practice

The introduction to this section of the module is approached through discussion within the lecture sessions, building from individuals to pairs, then fours or fives to report to the whole group. Basic definitions are taught this way, encouraging the students to build upon their own ideas and experience, appreciate diversity of opinion, and come to understand specific terminology. The intention is that students should learn and appreciate the elementary relationships between ideas of invisibility and visibility; public and private spheres; reproduction and production; gender divisions in society, positions of power and patriarchy and relate these to spatial aspects of travel, employment opportunities and land use planning, and to some early thoughts on Feminist theory. Here the initial cartoon from Watkins, Rueda and Rodriguez (1992, p.3) is used as an introduction to Feminism; from this the ideas of learning and understanding 'a Geography *of* women' and of commitment to 'a Geography *for* women' are developed. Further theoretical ideas are left for deeper consideration in Part 2 optional modules. Cartoons are found to be stimulating resources for group discussions and may also be 're-used' later as 'data' response stimuli in structured questions in the end of semester examination.

The cartoons (Fig.1), published in *Teaching Geography* in 1984, form the title (with the significant quotation), and subsequent illustration in an editorial on geographical experiences in local areas in the school curriculum, and the need to show children 'wild country' areas to contrast with their home (often urban) localities. The emphasis is upon the value of fieldwork in such rural and often remote areas. (Editorial, 1984) The writer (the editor was male) makes no acknowledgement of the gendered (and other) stereotypes and bias (for example, the tradition of the male socialisation of fieldwork already mentioned - McDowell, 1992) within these cartoons. Indeed these remain an unmentioned element apart from one brief letter, by a woman, who pinpoints the issues directly and succinctly within the idea of a 'hidden curriculum' favouring males, in the subsequent journal issue (Lucas, 1984). No further comment on the cartoons, or reply to this letter, was published, or presumably submitted for publication. In the 1990s, such issues are more appreciated.

These cartoons are used as the commencement of the section on Gender - 'Why study gender?' - within the Year one foundation module in Human Geography. The student group comprises mainly white school leavers (often with a majority of males) with a small number of mature entrants. Many wish to read Geography as a major subject to 'Finals' level. A few may be taking Women's Studies as a Minor or Joint. The students are provided with copies of the cartoons, simultaneously shown on the overhead projector, and the questions in Table 3.

Geography in the Wilderness

'The question is not what you look at, but what you see'
Henry David Thoreau *(1817-62)*

Figure 1

© Teaching Geography, April 1984

They are asked, without any priming apart from the session title, to answer questions 1/2, first as individuals, without consulting their peers, and then to discuss their answers in groups of two or three neighbours in the lecture. These sub-groups are then asked to contribute their ideas to the group as a whole.

The results have shown similar characteristics since this module commenced four years ago. Most students see the cartoons as representative of fieldwork - nothing more. Only a few (usually less than 5%), and predominantly the adult entrants and/or those who have studied Sociology or Women's Studies before coming to college, see the explicit gendered inequality in the group of pupils, staff member, and in the activities of all those portrayed.

Consideration of these cartoons leads on to a reading of two passages, one from the first edition of a specified Geography text (Haggett, 1972, pp.1-2) and the other from the revised third edition of the same book, (Haggett, 1979, p.3) in which non-sexist language is adopted.

There is a mixed appreciation by the students of the content of these extracts. The two exercises lead to a discussion of gender issues in Human Geography and are used to introduce particular basic issues and elements of a Feminist approach. These are here related to characteristics of students' learning experiences within Human Geography.

The further example of travel, accessibility and mobility studies provides appreciation of gender based work in the module's content and teaching and learning strategies and practice.

Table 3
Consider the attached cartoons carefully.

1.
a) Comment on the cartoons; what are your _immediate_ reactions?

....

b) any _further_ reactions?

....

2. In the light of 1a/b, would you redraw these cartoons?
    YES   NO   (Circle appropriate response)

    If <u>YES</u>, briefly describe the changes you would make from the originals.

....

The example of travel, accessibility and mobility

The work demonstrates the differing availability of different transport modes (especially the private car) to women compared with men - 'women are more reliant than men on public transport to meet their travel requirements.' (Pickup, 1988, p.98). Although the gender gap is diminishing, (Hill, 1996) women's relatively poor access to cars compared with that of men remains an important constraint upon women's trip making. This is exacerbated by the complexity of their typical journey patterns, still concerned with domestic functions of shopping, school, childcare, as well as increasingly paid employment, compared with men's often longer but much more straightforward daily journeys outward to work and return home. Moreover childcare responsibilities (Tivers, 1988) and care of elderly relatives continues to aggravate constraints upon women's travel opportunities compared with those of men (Bowlby, 1992).

Three main stimuli - a published diagram based upon academic research, a timetable and a cartoon - are used in teaching. The time-space approach is intended to demonstrate that constraints upon women's travel are a product of social roles of domesticity based on gender and the demands of these roles are felt through the interaction of variables of time and space. For example the temporal implications of taking children to and meeting them from school link with the resultant spatial implication of school location - of being required to be in a particular place at a specific time - and thus prevent being elsewhere at that time, with implications for other necessary appointments, employment. Whilst this approach has been criticised as being male-orientated (for instance it does tend to emphasise activities outside the home, i.e. public rather than private) (Rose, 1993), it does stimulate student thought about everyday activity patterns and the effects of varying opportunities (e.g. of changing opening hours of shops, part time employment opportunities, changing transport services/car ownership). Thus students are asked to discuss Moseley's diagram for 'a rural housewife' (1979), compare this with the position of the elderly, children, the disabled in combination with class/race/gender aspects and with that of themselves - for the latter they are asked to draw up a diary of their activities for a 'typical' weekday, and compare it in discussion with that of other students. This is related to the problems of those reliant upon public transport and uses a cartoon (TEST/FoE, 1984) and a timetable, both for rural areas, which compare appropriately with Moseley's diagram. Urban areas are included in discussion.

Table 4 shows the abbreviated coach service (once a week) within a rural county in Britain. It is based upon an actual example but the place names are fictitious. Catbury and Dogborough are small market centres, main foci for shopping and employment. The bus service is of the type often found in rural areas - one bus a week each way linking main towns and intermediate settlements. Students are asked to consider the position of a woman living on Thrush Hill, Much Growling. First they assume that she has two young children and requires a buggy/pram to transport one of them and no car available, since her partner takes their single car (for which she has a valid driving licence) to

Table 4
Catbury - Dogborough Coach services (Thursdays only)

	depart	arrive
Catbury bus station	08.57	13.02
Much Growling (Thrush Hill)	09.40	12.19
Much Growling (School)	09.42	12.17
Much Growling (Lower Ground)	09.44	12.16
Dogborough bus station	10.09	11.50
	(outward)	(return)

work each day, and secondly that she is elderly, widowed and living alone. They are asked to bear in mind that Thrush Hill is a very steep walk uphill from Lower Ground! Also, the small supermarket in Dogborough centre is 1,000 metres walk from the bus station and further larger facilities are available in a new shopping centre outside Dogborough, for which one would have to change buses. This work leads to more sophisticated analyses of accessibility issues for women in Part Two modules.

Student evaluation

Formal evaluation of the Year one Geography course is conducted through a long established computer based questionnaire, which covers breadth rather than detailed content sections of specific modules. Unless students feel very strongly about a particular aspect, specific study themes tend not to appear in student responses. In 1996 for example there is one mention of Equal Opportunities, nothing for gender which again reinforces the conventional concern of Geography. This evaluation does not provide staff with *fine-detailed* views of module content, nor does it stimulate student consideration of these; it is not intended to do so.

It was thus appropriate to introduce more specifically student views of the gender/Women's Studies content of the Human Geography module as evaluation of three years of teaching and development. This was done through a further questionnaire, brief and to the point, issued to the student group without warning immediately after the Easter break during the first session of the Summer Term 1996, a time when it was hoped that there had been an opportunity to reflect upon the module's content. The element of surprise was intended to facilitate an immediate personal response, assuming that such timing would give a genuine sample of student feeling rather than a longer preparation period.

Table 5
Year One Human Geography
Geography and Gender

Please answer the following questions:

1   Before you came to Edge Hill, had you studied gender/women's issues in a Geography course?
        YES   NO

    If 'Yes', please state examination board ....
    and level of course (GCSE, 'A' level, etc) ....

2   Before you came to Edge Hill, had you studied gender/women's issues in any course except Geography?

        YES   NO

    If 'Yes', please state
    (i)   level of course(s)   ....
    (ii) Examination board   ....
    (iii) subject(s)   ....

3   After discussing gender/women's issues in this module what is your view of their place in Human Geography? (Please write no more than two sentences.)

4   Please give any further advantages and/or disadvantages you see in the study of gender relations in Geography:
    (a) Advantages:

    (b) Disadvantages:

5   Please indicate your sex: F   M
    and your age if over 18 when you started your college course : ......

The questionnaire (Table 5) comprises two broad functional types of questions, (i) seeking factual information about the individual, and (ii) requesting opinions and ideas about the study of gender relations/women's issues within the Human Geography module. The former include details of previously acquired studies of gender/women's issues in a Geography (Q.1) or other (Q.2) course, seeking level of course, subject and examination board, details of the individual's gender, and age - whether the respondent was a 'typical' school leaver of circa eighteen years on commencing the module in September 1995, or whether s/he was 'mature' - the latter were asked to give their ages (Q.5). These questions are intended to provide an individual anonymous profile of each student, and a composite for the group, and to establish specific 'social and educational' sub-groups within and between which to analyse and compare results. 'Closed' questions are used for precision in seeking such basic factual information. Students' opinions and views of the study area were sought through more 'open' questions, allowing the students to voice their own ideas of the place of gender/Women's Studies issues in Human Geography (Q.3) with a more specified prompt towards further advantages and disadvantages of these studies in Q.4. The initial question aimed to allow students to speak for themselves, the latter to focus more closely upon specific directions of viewpoint. In the event this structure did provide material which related together, and gave students a foundation (Q.3) which they could develop as/if they wished in Q.4.

The student profile

The sample number of questionnaires completed was thirty six, twenty two (61%) of whom were female and fourteen (39%) male. Eight students (22%) were 'mature', ranging from twenty to thirty four years of age. The average age of 'mature' females was 25.5 years; that of males was 25.25 years. A minority of the group had studied gender/women's issues previous to coming to Edge Hill University College. Only one (male) had encountered such material in an 'A' level (NEAB) Geography course; twelve students (33.3% of the sample) had discovered gender/Women's Studies in other courses of varying examination boards - seven in Sociology, two in Communications Studies, one in each of English literature and English language (all 'A' level) and one in History GCSE (SEG). From the onset of teaching material on women and other social groups within this module, it had been anticipated that students would have little background to such work from their previous Geography courses, and that only some would have experienced studies of women's issues through other disciplinary approaches. The questionnaire returns confirm that these expectations and the adoption of a 'no assumed previous knowledge' approach in teaching are appropriate for Year One Geography groups at present. One looks forward to a more gender-informed Human Geography at GCSE and 'A' levels to follow the lead of other social sciences, and of increasing numbers of academics who appreciate gender issues.

Student views and opinions of module content

The responses to the 'open' questions 3 and 4 of the questionnaire are analysed at two levels. In broad summary terms the responses to Q.3 ('After discussing gender/women's issues in this module, what is your view of their place in Human Geography?') are overwhelmingly positive (circa 78% of the sample) with only two candidates (5.5%) negative. The remaining six candidates (16.5%) suggest positive elements tempered by negative conditions. This summary is based solely upon what students have written, i.e. it does not seek to challenge at this stage their opinions and views by further analysis of the content of their ideas such as bias and political correctness (below). The invitation to assert 'any further advantages and/or disadvantages ... in the study of gender relations in Geography' (Q.4) produced twenty three responses for advantages (64% of the sample), i.e. expansion of positive views in Q.3, and twenty one responses on disadvantages (58%), complementing the ideas of the two candidates above.

In detail, the responses display a thought provoking variety of ideas and themes, particularly after a broad foundation module concerned with other issues as well as gender. Many are gratifying in their appreciation of the intentions of the teaching, or in a smaller number, produce concern over misunderstandings still apparent in some of the students' reception of the material. Popular misconceptions, doubts, contradictions and stereotypes characterise some of these views and suggest further strengthening and targeting of teaching to overcome these limitations in future years.

As indicated, *positive responses* dominate the total data given by the students. 'Positive' is interpreted here as perceiving value, advantage, benefit, in the incorporation of gender/women's issues in Human Geography, i.e. they are supportive of the Feminist content and interpretations as taught. These positive comments can be grouped into seven distinctive, inter-linking classes :

(i) Those which identify a general/societal relevance;
(ii) Those which highlight an increase in personal awareness through these studies;
(iii) Those which specify issues of equality and the invisibility of women;
(iv) Those which recognise the importance of integrating women's issues into Human Geography;
(v) Those which identify the need for new (Feminist) concepts in Human Geography;
(vi) Those which appreciate the research potential of studies of gender/women's in Human Geography;
(vii) Those which value gender/women's issues in linking together associated academic disciplines.

Eight students (29% of the positive responses) identify general and societal relevance although one of these also counters these positive attributes by negative points. (discussed below) Candidates specify general aspects such as 'disadvantage facing females in society', bias within society, and several relate to personal experience and appreciation of inequality: 'I feel, as a female, that it makes a point of us being different, and therefore at a disadvantage. We should not be.' Such comments link closely with a growing individual awareness - 'It's given me a good insight into the biases of society towards women and issues of gender in the world today' is one example - and link personal development with a perception of the group's and society's needs. These five student views are intentionally ordered to represent a progression of increasing realisation of an approach to feminism as a way towards greater understanding and appreciation of society as a whole than is acknowledged within a patriarchal system:

> Gives an insight into women's views and experiences;
> Makes people more aware, particularly males;
> Shows people's ignorance, and in some cases, "bigotry" (sic);
> Gets across views of everyone;
> Allows all views to be considered.

In particular, issues of equality and inequality, visibility and invisibility are demonstrated. Twenty students (71%) assert that the advocacy of gender studies in Human Geography aids the greater visibility of women, 'increased awareness of issues needing to be highlighted', such as accessibility, work location, schools, housing, and of 'inequalities in gender', showing 'problems encountered by both females and males in society' and 'the role and importance of equality for women in society'. The heightening of awareness of these issues is again recognised by several respondents.

Within this general learning and societal context, students developed considerable support for the incorporation and studies of gender/women's issues within Human Geography. Nineteen responses (68%) gave strong advocacy, exemplified by 'gender issues can be integrated well in geographical thinking' and 'women play an essential role in human activity and they have a relevant place in Human Geography'. Again many students show a clear appreciation of the stimulation of their personal development and growing awareness: women's issues 'should have a place in Human Geography. However, I didn't realise this until after studying it within Human Geography'; 'it has made me personally more aware at how biased society is towards women'. A small minority of the group took the academic implications for Geography more deeply, two in particular recognising the importance of gender/Women's Studies both 'to provide a further concept to that of Human Geography', and a further that the 'role in Geography though new to the classroom is an interesting area for research'. It is also pleasing that two different students emphasised the breadth and relevance of knowledge across traditional academic boundaries, appreciating links between Women's Studies and other degree programmes in college as well as Geography - urban policy studies (with which Geography has two different joint pathways) and applied social science - and in the integration of 'various social science subjects'.

'Mixed' responses demonstrate positive comments linked with above, but show a degree of caution, doubt, apprehension, and perhaps a fear of ideas new to the individuals, ones of which they might be partly convinced on one hand, but do not have the confidence or conviction to fully honour without particular reservations. It may be that they feel unable to embrace completely Feminist ideas, given their past and present perception of prevailing views and attitudes and the reflection of these in their studies, especially in Geography, preceding higher education. Hence positive views are tempered by comments such as 'some aspects of "politically correct statements" were not needed', or reflecting perhaps a fear of the unknown, of how far new ideas will lead: 'Women have a relevant place in Human Geography but I feel the topic goes too deep'; 'I feel gender issues are important as long as the issues are not dragged to the extremes and made ridiculous'. The values placed implicitly upon depth, 'the extremes', and 'ridiculous' suggest a very real fear of straying from the students' accepted 'straight and narrow' conceptual and factual traditional (geographical) boundaries of study without suggesting, knowing or justifying what these boundaries should be. This is further augmented by the explicit use of words maintaining existing patriarchal hierarchies expressed by the assertion, 'I think that women should have an equal role in society, but I don't agree that men should be suppressed to advance this'. Sadly the ideas of fostering equality and equal opportunities as a relevant attribute of a Feminist approach are lost in this statement, as indeed they are in the weakness of commitment expressed by 'I believe it to be only a minor issue although it can be seen that females are not taken into consideration sometimes'.

It is so too with *negative responses*, which further demonstrate these fears and prejudices of the unknown of extending ideas and recognition of gender and women's issues across traditional societal and subject boundaries, and which indicate a perception of these giving little or no added value, advantage or benefit to Human Geography. Seven groups of problems are identified by these students, mostly as a response to Q.4, which opened up the idea of disadvantages of the approach. Issues raised encompass:

(i) General/societal considerations;
(ii) Problems of bias, and perceptions of bias;
(iii) Generation of controversy;
(iv) Depth of study;
(v) Relevance of study;
(vi) Generation of pressure upon women;
(vii) Problems of political correctness.

Two statements on general considerations suggest 'far too much importance put on the issue' neglecting 'broader issues i.e. should not be central focus in higher education but part of it' or more specifically because 'we did lots of work on women's problems but surely men have problems as well which should be addressed'. The latter point is not denied, but fails to appreciate the traditional concentration of Geography upon the public realm, and men's issues. Nine students remark upon bias. In a general sense they are worried that ' lectures may tend to be biased'. Some are more specific about their fears of bias against men - 'devalues the male issues' and its assumed result, 'could bias males' - or bias towards women - 'too much emphasis could be placed on just the "women" aspect'; 'maybe seen as looking more at women's issues, and less at men's' without appreciating that this would be a corrective to the long existing male centred bias in much traditional work. Indeed the bias of much academic work towards a male viewpoint, male actions, and a male world, with its inherent dangers of retaining and enhancing male power and dominance is not recognised in these responses. This is a disappointing evaluation by these students, of a module in which critical assessment of the invisibility of women in much Human Geography and of the unrepresentative nature of studying only 'half of the human in Human Geography' (Monk & Hanson, 1982) was encouraged and discussed. Such apprehension among respondents links with a fear of creating controversy in two responses: 'can evoke "heated discussion" over the issues raised'; 'in some cases it may alienate male interest and participation in the classroom if too much opinion is voiced'. There are clear dangers for academic work if the discussion of opinions is stifled by a regard for male interests, without recognising that a preoccupation for men's affairs may well have discouraged women's interest and participation in past and present studies. Further comments that 'the study can be taken too far and can become too intense' or too deep, 'some studies seem to have been too extreme and I consider some of the concepts have been blown out of all proportions' mirror those above. They beg elucidation over the students' perception of scholarship, of wrestling with challenging, often difficult problems, as well as gender issues whose relevance is also questioned by one return. It is interesting that one student also considers that the incorporation of gender/Women's Studies into Geography will 'put more pressure ... on women'.

Political correctness also received comment: 'the only thing I worry about is sometimes it comes across as too "politically correct"'; '... scare people away through its overly aggressive attitude towards things close to people - such as the way they talk - chair, not chairman!'. Such ideas echo the influence of those who make sweeping comments in the media on Women's Studies without having any direct involvement within these studies. The result appears to be that some students assume that any studies of women's issues are political correctness alone, little if nothing more, and that such studies appear to offer a threat to individuals, culture and society alike (the establishment?), when indeed they should in reality enhance our knowledge and understanding of all three. For future teaching of this module it appears that these students need a further emphasis of the reasons for guidelines for writing already explained and based upon the ideas of Spender (1990) and the IBG guidelines (above).

Further analysis of the questionnaire responses is based upon the three profile characteristics of students: gender; age; previous knowledge of gender/women's issues through their school curricula. It might be expected that women's views of the gender content in the module might be more receptive than those of men, or that those with previous experience might be more favourable than those without. The sample is too small to show conclusive evidence of such trends. However the material is presented here for it is suggestive of certain ideas.

In the gender characteristic the sample has a 61%:39% female:male ratio, and it might be thought that this accounts for the generally positive response to Q.3. However the size of the majority indicates a positive response from men too although the negative responses were from women, and the mixed responses were overwhelmingly male (5:1 male:female). In Q.4 responses are equally divided between female and male. A more detailed check of negative responses similarly shows little difference between the sexes. In the categories identified above, the following female:male ratios (Table 6) are apparent. In this group gender has little role in explaining the responses to questions. Similarly the 'mature' students appear to show little discernible difference from the 'school leaver', entrants. Comparison of those students with previous (school curricula) experience of gender/women's issues with those without such experience are also non-conclusive - it is suggested that the sample is too small to allow meaningful analysis - although there are tendencies for those without previous knowledge to be more positive. the results are provided in Table 7. It must be recognised too that the sample was voluntary and is not a complete one. Many of those who did not respond are male; thus the sample is skewed towards the female views. However its anonymity and the use of 'open' questions have, it is considered, helped to derive a useful representation of student views.

Table 6

		F:M
General considerations		1:0
Bias		4:5
Controversy		0:1
Depth of study		2:3
Relevance		1:1
Pressure upon women		1:0
Political correctness		1:2
Other		1:0
	total:	11:12

Table 7

			% of sample group	% of whom female
Previous experience - 13 respondents				
Question 3		positive	69	67
		negative	8	100
		mixed	23	67
Question 4		(a) advantages	0	-
		(b) disadvantages	10	100
		(c) both	90	67
No previous experience - 23 respondents				
Question 3		positive	83	68
		negative	0	-
		mixed	17	0
Question 4		(a) advantages	20	67
		(b) disadvantages	7	0
		(c) both	73	57

Conclusions

Whilst the subject matter is exciting and relevant, and stimulates a depth of commitment and enthusiasm in teaching, one of the greatest challenges in introducing Geography students to issues of, and for women, is the students' perception of the credibility of such work in their own lives and in Human Geography. Initially many are sceptical at best. Others, female and male, have proved vocally hostile, and one suspects some 'vote with their feet' so as not to face the demands of trying to think in new ways, either by not attending the taught sessions or by taking very little part except where directly involved through discussion/answers, and avoiding reading and assessment relating to these issues for those to which they are more accustomed in Geography courses at school - GCSE and 'A' levels. Thankfully this is not true of the majority and evaluation does demonstrate that many students do attempt to grasp these challenges and find their thoughts broadened, engendered and enriched. What is required is dialogue between Geography school examination boards and an incorporation of gender/women's issues into Geography syllabuses. Critics who suggest knowledge is being 'downgraded' fail to appreciate the value of new (to commence 1996-7) GCSE syllabuses in Geography which 'concentrate on testing students' knowledge of social, gender and ethnic issues'. (Scott-Clark, 1996).

At EHUC the work in Year One on gender and Feminist Geography is a foundation for studies of Feminist method in the Year Two Human Geography practical module and for the optional Part 2 module (open to Women's Studies and Geography students) in Feminist Geography. The latter is popular, attracting male as well as female students and their evaluations are heartening. The possibility of completing a dissertation in Feminist Geography is now more realistic, given this foundation of taught experience, and an increasing literature in Feminist Geography, and in Geography texts including gender/women's issues. (e.g. Sibley, 1995) These latter contrast with volumes that still avoid Feminist issues, maintaining the traditional invisibility, or include them as tokens of acknowledgement.

In Geography teaching and research in higher education, much depends upon individual efforts in developing and extolling Feminist Geography, still seen as a minority interest. This picture appears international whether in advanced countries such as Australia and New Zealand (Johnson, 1989), Britain (Bowlby, 1992), Germany (Binder, 1989), the Netherlands (Karsten, 1989), or in the developing nations such as India (Raju and Satish, 1989) or Taiwan (Chiang, 1989). The situation is not helped by financial and resourcing pressures upon universities nor by 'domination by men' and in some areas, 'physical Geography' (Chiang, 1989), and traditional views . Bowlby, (1989) however concludes 'that the fundamental importance of the subject - concerned as it is with the subordination of half the world's population - will ensure its survival', and that 'the prospects for Feminist Geography in Britain are exciting'.

Students pick up this excitement. Susan Hanson's description of the reaction of a postgraduate student to Feminist teaching is illustrative:

> One of my male PhD students recently gave a seminar... he sees himself as a Feminist now - and he said when he came to Clark he never even thought about feminism or been exposed to it in an academic setting ... But he started working on our research project ... and he said that being thrown in at the deep end of this research, as well as daily interaction with other Feminists in the department, opened up his mind to new ways of thinking. (McDowell, 1994, p.25).

Similarly undergraduates at EHUC have voiced similar new found commitment, voiced in their evaluation of the Feminist Geography components in Year one (above) and Part two modules:

> Really interesting course, teaching something that I was not personally aware of prior to the course. Nice one!

7 Women's Studies/Media Studies changing perspectives: a case study

Angela Thew and Carol Poole

The continuous transformations that are occurring in Women's Studies and Media Studies force us to re-examine tools of analysis, especially concepts and methodologies. These transformations oblige us at the same time to look at fundamental questions in relation to teaching and learning in Higher Education. This chapter describes the developments of the 'real' life experience of the writers in course design and delivery of a module *Women and the Media* for final year Women's Studies undergraduates.

We both felt something special about working on a project that was particularly designed for women and their relationship to the media. We welcomed the challenge! We saw the project as a real opportunity to discuss some of the issues which had been troubling us in media studies concerning women in a media-saturated culture and their position in new post-modern discourses. However, we had a course to design and a curriculum to plan, and of equal importance were current debates about teaching and learning in higher education and issues relating to development of transferable skills. In curriculum planning we found ourselves falling back on a few longstanding models which we felt were still very useful as a 'rule of thumb'. Our model involved addressing aims, objectives, content, method, assessment and evaluation.

To address this fully we needed to consider current debates in teaching and learning in higher education today. Entwistle (1992) discusses more effective ways to achieve 'traditional goals' in teaching in higher education which tend to focus on content and are subject specific. He also examines current debates which are critical of the narrow academic approach to teaching and learning in higher education which, he says, can lead to 'passive learning': many degree programmes are loaded with detailed information which is often assessed within a narrow academic context. The emphasis is too much on academic content at the expense of other skills which might equip students to cope more fully in the real world.

Employers have also complained that graduates do not possess many of the skills they require, for example: ability to work collaboratively; good inter-personal and communication skills and positive attitudes towards business and industry. Through initiatives like the Enterprise in Higher Education (EHE) employers have suggested that these additional 'transferable skills' should be developed in the context of higher education.

These ideas are, of course, well tried and tested in Further Education. Both writers have considerable experience in delivery of vocational curriculum in Further Education, which has fostered development of these skills over many years. One of the writers is currently managing an Open Learning Unit and has many years experience developing curriculum and resources for open and flexible learning environments which offer a range of teaching learning experiences.

The one semester long *Women and the Media* module could be used to introduce some innovations and hopefully over time others might be introduced. We felt right away that we could certainly incorporate some 'transferable skills' aims into our programme as these principles are fairly easily put into practice via open-ended project work. This we had already agreed upon and it would be done in negotiation with the students. After much discussion and deliberations we agreed on the following set of aims:

1. To engage students in a critical debate about the discourses which structure the mediation of women in the world.
2. To provide an analytical approach to signs and meaning and the institutional, social and historical conditions which govern the semiotic structure of discourse.
3. To provide students with a framework upon which to engage in current debates.
4. To engage students in collaborative project work which would demonstrate their ability to work as a member of a team and exercise their inter-personal and communications skills.

Once we had agreed our aims we were able to concentrate our minds on our objectives, these would come from a step by step breakdown of how the students would achieve the course aims.

As this was only a one-semester module, we had very limited time to achieve ambitious aims. We needed to know the profile of the students in so far as it was possible. This involved questions regarding students' prior learning. With finite time and resources and a very broad course content which would be required to fulfill the aims, we could not afford to waste time or resources covering ground students had already trodden elsewhere. We felt that a good course content through which we could attain our objectives should not only be based around what the lecturer would do but primarily what the women on the course would be doing. In addressing their needs we agreed we must be as student-centred and as interactive as possible and that we would address this more thoroughly in our teaching methodology. We also felt we should try to develop approaches in ourselves that would encourage what has been described as a 'deep' rather than 'surface' level of learning which would engage students in a broader, more analytical, approach to the subject.

Once we had profiled our target group we knew we were dealing with third year degree level students, coming from a range of disciplines. We then needed to address what we might take for granted. All students would have successfully achieved passes on several modules on the Women's Studies Programme and would be well versed in the up-to-date Feminist debates in the broadest cultural context. We felt that while we might expect one or two of the students to have some communications, media or cultural studies background, we could not generally assume such knowledge and that we would need to be more explicit and thoroughgoing in our exposition of these subject areas and in explaining what level of knowledge and understanding we would expect. For what it was worth at this stage we took a look at our own knowledge and experience. What, for example, was our (her) story of events which we would inevitably be relating to the students? What also were the discourses in the area of media and how did these discourses relate to the story of modern Feminism? All of this we knew would inform our content and influence our aims and objectives. We felt that it might be useful, in our introductory session, to give the students a short biography of ourselves which might indicate to them where our personal biases might lie which the students would be able to take into account in the course delivery.

Media and Cultural studies are progressive in their theoretical approaches. Over a number of decades we, as Feminists, have had to adapt painfully to certain new perspectives. As one traditional and one not-so-traditional marxist we have faced some political and academic dilemmas which can be contentious in the area of Media and Cultural studies and even more so in Women's Studies. The questions thrown up as a result of current post-modern debates can ultimately undermine the collective approach which has been essential, in our view, to the strength and success of the Women's Movement. As Feminists from a marxist tradition, patriarchy to us had been entirely explicable as the result of class-based capitalism in which males had economic power and therefore control over females because of that power. Post-fifties Feminist politics and philosophy have been particularly important to many media theorists in explaining theories of commodity fetishism and an analysis of the culture industries in modern capitalism which sell representations of women as commodity products based around certain cultural stereotypes.

What, however, makes current debate different, and therefore challenging, is the decline in the grand or meta-narrative explanations of 'reality'. This takes the debates into a whole new dimension. How do women cope with the decline of the grand narrative which has been so useful in their collective political action on the one hand and on the other does this new fragmentation and more liberalist and individualist bias, which informs current debate, reflect more fully the 'real' lives of women?

It seemed appropriate to us to open up the debate with reference to ideology, cultural discourses and modern culture, highlighting the importance of the Frankfurt School. Although this perspective is now outdated, it is crucial in explaining what followed subsequently in semiology. We can also use the School's critique of consumer capitalism, marxism and the failure of Enlightenment thinking; how they saw the use of the mass media as an instrument for a mass subjugation even though a mass manipulation approach is now considered over-simplistic. It is also useful to look at many of the figures involved in the School after the war who developed more liberal social science paradigms in order to introduce other political and Feminist perspectives. While a liberal Feminism might criticise unequal and exploitative employment and representation of women in the media this perspective only argues for remedial equal opportunities legislation to rectify the situation. We might here debate the role history has played in demonstrating control and repression of women in patriarchy. We would expect the students to be familiar with and bring to the debate various Feminist discourses. These would include views that women and men might indeed be so completely divergent that we might need to question the usefulness of the patriarchal paradigms we are currently using to analyse the role of women in patriarchy.

In introducing ideology McLennan's (1991) account is a good starting point. In *The Power of Ideology* he sets out three conditions for ideology to exist:

1. The ideas concerned must be shared by a significant number of people.
2. The ideas must form some kind of coherent system.
3. The ideas must connect in some way to the use of power in society.

As ideology expresses itself through discourse it was considered that time spent in this area would be useful and add to the student's knowledge and experience. An awareness by students of the nature and function of cultural discourses as never pure and innocent and as determinants of the socially constructed ways of representing women was felt to be a necessary introduction to the subject. Cultural discourses are constructed from various strands of ideology. Such expression is a way of making the ideology social. At this point we thought it might be useful to analyse attitudes, values and beliefs within a specific culture. We would ask students if in looking at representations of women in the media, they can discern any of the attitudes, values and beliefs found towards women in a western culture, bearing in mind the models of politics, economics and society we had discussed so far. We would also ask how these representations of women might be different placed in different ideological and cultural discourses, for example, African and Muslim cultures. We also questioned ideology as a concept and the nature of its existence as this is doubted by some theorists.

Before looking at the influence of semiotic analysis in the deconstruction of representations of women in media we felt that linked to the social, economic, cultural and sexual discourses discussed it might be useful to address the producers of representations of women or more broadly the institutions, and concepts of ownership and control. In looking at institutions we would raise issues related around what Corner (1991), Ang & Hermes (1988) and others label, in their various ways, the public and private domains. Emphasis here would be on the public role of women in relation to the place and production in media industries. We would also use comparative analysis based on the specific research Angela Thew has been doing in relation to the British and Canadian experiences and how both countries are tackling the position of women working and producing in the media industries.

Later we would include the role of women represented in the private sphere in relation to media consumption when we would have an opportunity to examine specific research in the areas of film, television, magazines and so on. However before we could be effective in examining women in these specific areas we would need to be armed with a little more theory or should we say methodology. For this we must turn to the influence of structuralism and semiology and its limits in relation to the creation of meaning.

We felt we must emphasise the importance of semiology as a method in the analysis of women in the media, especially in film. However it is also important to emphasise that while it is and has been an important methodological approach it is by no means the only approach and has recently been criticised. For this reason we felt we should present it as a methodology. Here we would also need to introduce students to other methodological approaches. These include content analysis and ideology used in, for example, the works of McRobbie (1978), when looking at girls' magazines, and interview and questionnaire techniques used by Ien Ang (1989), in her work on Dallas and that of Joke Hermes (1995) in researching women's magazine reading.

However, we felt again that given the time and resource constraints it would be sufficient to brush over many of the methods of gathering information about the media especially in the quantitative category. Third year students on a Women's Studies degree programme should have come across sufficient research using quantitative methodology. Our concentration, we thought, should be on the qualitative methodology, particularly semiotics, and we would outline only briefly quantitative methods of analysis and back that outline up with supporting materials. The bulk of our time we would, therefore, spend on the exposition and application of structuralism and semiology in its theory, method and practice. This would serve a number of purposes: firstly it would fill in the gaps which might exist in the students' knowledge; secondly it indicates the importance and significance of the application of semiotics to the area of representation in the media; and thirdly it would act as a useful point of departure for introducing other more quantitative approaches which are again becoming popular especially in audience research. These centre the reader rather than text.

However, there is no question that structuralism and semiology, both of which came into prominence in the 1950s have left their mark on Feminism, through their concepts and procedures of signs, signifiers, signified and decoding and still continue to be used in the analysis of women in the media especially in the private domain of popular culture. Here, although we would introduce a number of theorists, for example Pierce, Saussure Strauss and even Eco, given time constraints we would need to concentrate on the work of Roland Barthes. Emphasis here would be on Barthes' idea that reality is always constructed, and made intelligible to human understanding by culturally specific systems of meaning.

At this stage students would need to be armed with background information in relation to codes and conventions used in the various media and how they might change and develop over time if they are to apply semiological analysis. Here we would focus in more closely to analyse such codes as used for example in film, television, newspaper and magazines, advertising and so on. Students would also be given opportunity in workshops to apply these methods in practice.

Finally, before going on to look more specifically at the various debates in a number of chosen areas, which we would be able to research more closely, we would need to go back to the point we made above about semiology as a point of departure for looking more closely at the reader as the pivotal point from which to study women in the media. To do this we would give the students a brief historical perspective from which they can analyse developments and make philosophical links between grand narrative perspectives and current post-modern ones. To do this we need again to briefly refer students back to the Frankfurt School and mass manipulation theory, through the two-step flow model onto uses and gratifications models popular with women researchers. In this research we can see a clear shift in emphasis from the collective to the individual reader of the text. This of course also demands other and various political discourses and contexts. We need to look closely at the work of Morley and the *Nationwide Study* (1980) and Ang's book *Desperately seeking the Audience* (1991) and the earlier works such as that of Hobson (1982) and work on soaps by Fiske (1987) and most interestingly the post-modern approach adopted by Joke Hermes (1995) in studying the reading of women's magazines in Britain and the Netherlands.

We felt that, given the students' prior learning experiences together with the new theoretical and methodological frameworks they were now studying, they should be reasonably well armed in the area of media and cultural studies to progress to some more in-depth research. We also felt that we could achieve delivery of the above content in about five lectures, although a couple more would have been appreciated had time permitted. We should now move on to look in depth at research and debates in a number of specific areas. However, as the course was only one semester with a final session for assessment there was a serious time problem. The first five sessions were essential to building up background knowledge, theory and methodology and presenting an overview so that we could assume a fairly equal distribution of knowledge and understanding of the subject among the students. This would ensure a minimum standard of quality assurance in terms of the student's approach in successfully attaining the learning objectives. Our penultimate session would be an assessment and our final session would be to bring together and relate to the students our thematic approach and ask them to evaluate the course. This would leave us with only three more available sessions. We also knew that we required at least one session to discuss Feminism, deconstruction and the post-modern debates, which then just left two sessions.

We felt we would really only now be getting into the subject and realised that one semester was just not long enough, but we could do nothing about it on this run of the course. We felt we had now armed the students with the tools to do the job but they would not be able to apply them broadly enough to specific situations. Some students of course might choose to do assignments on work we had already covered, but those who wanted to key into a specific area of research such as television, newspapers, advertising, new technology and the Internet, would be disappointed as at this time we would only be able to cover two specific areas. At this point we were over five weeks into the course and were able to ask students for their preferences in relation to specific areas for research. It was agreed that we would look at women in film and women in magazines.

For film we looked at works from that of Haskell (1973), Kaplan (1983), Kuhn (1982), Brunsdon (1986) and Mulvey (1975). The later discusses patriarchy in Hollywood via visual codes again seeing man as the active bearer of the gaze and woman as the passive object. Through the agency of the camera gaze the male and the female are encouraged to look with the man using Freud's Oedipal trajectory. Here looking at woman is thought to bring on a fear of castration in the man and therefore the pleasure of looking is undermined by fear. This fear Mulvey feels is handled by voyeurism and fetishism in which the male may be taking sadistic pleasure. Obviously we address current criticisms of the male gaze. For example the fact of male dominance here might simply be related to the fact that they have dominance in terms of ownership and therefore control of media industries. We would also introduce concepts of the female gaze and look at the work of Gamman and Marshment (1988) and others. The final vacant session we would dedicate to looking at the work of women magazines starting with McRobbie (1978) on *Jackie* which shows women as objects in patriarchy, and the work of Winship (1987). We also introduce Frazer's (1990) and Michael's criticisms of content analysis.

We move on from text centred analysis and look at some audience-centred approaches starting with the work of Hobson (1982) and the reaction by other Feminists to the psychoanalytical approaches based on the Althussarian/Lacan paradigm in which spectator positioning implies a subjection to the text's inherent power. The psychoanalytic version here seems to treat the symbolic as the only dimension of power and has been ignoring reception and ideological effects of film. If we adopt the Althusarian/Lacan model we would believe that Hollywood is solely responsible for positioning of capitalist subjects. Of course we are never telling students what to think but presenting the debates as fully as possible.

Today this model is still defended but we also look at the work of those women who have sought to modify the model: Lauretis (1984), Williams (1987) and Modleski (1988). Reception theory is also important. It is much more complex than had been previously thought. Many researchers, Ang, Hermes and so on, are finding, as did Hobson, evidence of the pleasure women get from their reading of the text; and that women are discriminating in their reading competence. Of course much of this work owes something to Morley (1980) and we need to look closely again at audience. It would have been excellent to go on to look at television and melodrama but unfortunately we had run out of time.

In our final session before presentation of project work and assessment we pulled together our themes and ideas before final evaluation. We needed at this point to address the issues already discussed regarding women in a so-called post modern culture. In our final session we looked at Feminist scholarship based in Enlightenment thinking and what Nicholson (1990, p.3) calls 'a God's eye view' as opposed to that which expressed the perspectives of particular persons or groups. This session aims to question '... claims about the inevitable "situatedness" of human thought within culture to focus on the very criteria by which claims to knowledge are legitimised'. We would here question whether or not postmodernism might be destructive of Feminism as Feminism might, in fact, depend on the social construction of 'woman' which, as Nicholson points out, is a notion post-modernism would attack. Could it be that post-modern ideas have arrived conveniently when woman is now becoming much more 'centred' and man can afford to be more 'decentred'. Of course, we do not aim to answer such large questions, but we do aim to broaden the debate and hopefully make it more interesting to our students.

Assessment

Assessment of the module would be through a specific written assignment of 1,500 words and a presentation by groups of two or three members. Presentations would be negotiated between students and lecturers. Students would be encouraged to make full use of the range of media equipment available to them such as video, television, OHP and slides. They would also be encouraged to make appointments outside of the sessions for advice and guidance on their project work. It was noted at the end of the course that those students who did take full advantage of the tutorial facility did much better in their presentations. Lecturers' perceptions were that during this process students had been able to consolidate their learning further and apply it more strategically.

Evaluation

The delivery of the module tended towards the theoretical rather than the descriptive. It was felt that in these days of instructional technology and computer-based learning, a mapping of the subject area was a more appropriate delivery method and students should fill in detailed accounts of theories covered as demanded by their specific requirements.

Students were initially put off by this approach and expressed this in verbal evaluations which took place after sessions. Evaluation also showed that some students had misconceptions as to what the course would be about before starting. The lecturers' perceptions were that students had expected to see numerous media portrayals of poor defenceless women for discussion. This is an approach both lecturers wanted to avoid as it was felt to be unnecessary and to some extent gratuitous. It was decided to use such images with economy and only to back up a very serious academic point in deconstructing power relations within cultural discourse. This is something students did begin to appreciate as the course progressed.

Tutors also took for granted that students on their third year of a degree programme in Women's Studies would be able to handle a more theoretical approach to the subject even if they had not studied the media before, although it was accepted that most students would and did find it difficult and expressed concerns which seemed to disappear as confidence in dealing with the theoretical aspects grew.

Considerations and Conclusion

After the first run of the course it materialised that a number of issues would have to be addressed for future runs. It was felt that too much ground was covered in the space of one semester. Overloading a syllabus, in the view of the lecturers can lead to what Entwistle (1992) calls a 'surface' approach to learning which tutors wished to avoid. To develop a 'deeper' approach it would be necessary to increase the time spent in delivery and consolidation of the material.

In their self assessment, lecturers also felt that in delivering the course they must work even harder to simplify extremely complex ideas and make them more accessible to students in 'real life' contexts. They also felt that in the long term they should work towards achieving a more open and flexible approach to the delivery of the material, apply teaching strategies which would promote a 'deeper' learning experience.

Developments of the project we feel should address approaches to more flexible teaching methods. Given the reasonably small intake, interactive teaching has so far been possible. However, institutional practices are such that small group teaching cannot be guaranteed and future runs of the module could necessitate a complete revision of methodology because of large student numbers. This year we have experienced conflict between institutional provision and our teaching practice in that we have been allocated a lecture theatre which is not conducive to interactive teaching and although our numbers could accommodate an inter-active approach our spatial parameters do not!

8 'Exiting the symbols' A discussion of the role and practice of Drama in the teaching of Women's Studies

Elizabeth Hare

My title is chosen from a phrase used by Sue Ellen Case (1995) to describe the contribution made to Feminist theory and theatre by Helene Cixous, the French Feminist theorist. My thesis echoes hers in that it describes the necessity for women to exit from the male construct of female performance if we are to make a performance art that is truly ours and to create our own canon of works within it. This idea lies at the heart of the way in which the course 'Women and Performance' is constructed and delivered. Also central is the relationship between teaching Drama and teaching Women's Studies and the relationship that exists between Feminism and theatre. This is turn highlights the way in which Feminist theory, and in particular, French Feminist theory, informs the study of women's theatre.

The first task of the students registered on the course is to begin to construct a definition of women's performance and to set it against the ways in which men have constructed and defined women's performance in the past. In the first part of the chapter, I describe the development of these ideas and some of the sources which inform them. The final section of this chapter is devoted to a description of the practice of the teaching of the course and the sources that it draws on, and is followed by a critical analysis of the outcomes of that practice as I now perceive them having delivered the course twice.

The important interaction created by the existence of such a course between Women's Studies and the discipline of Drama is complex. There is a long tradition in the subject area of perceiving Drama as a useful medium for learning. This is traditionally one of the ways in which educational Drama is used in the school curriculum, as a cross curricular tool, as well as a subject in its own right. By allowing people to explore material in an active way, through the use of speech, action and the imagination, Drama allows for a particularly rich mode of learning, which is personal, allows the individual to gain insight, and interact in a creative way with a group. Drama as a mode of learning also promotes confidence, improves self esteem and provides participants with a clearer sense of their creative identity and potential and of their place in the culture. It is for all these reasons that Drama as a way of working has been so enormously successful with a wide range of disadvantaged groups, as may be witnessed in the work of Augusto Boal (1978).

These benefits are obviously entirely appropriate for students of Women's Studies who are concerned with consciousness raising and empowerment for themselves and others. However, Drama is also a subject and an art form in its own right. One of the benefits to students from other disciplines is that they are enabled to discover this for themselves and move away from the attitude prevailing in our culture, that the arts are generally of no use or benefit to anyone. Therefore a course of Drama in Women's Studies should provide both for a questioning of cultural prejudice and for the exploration of experience in dramatic form, and in this way the benefits of both the subject and of Drama as a learning medium can be fully enjoyed.

Within the artistic discipline and academic study of Drama and theatre, women's theatre has its own particular identity as outlined by the a number of theorists and evidenced and by practice in both the first and second women's liberation movements.

The sources for the course material

In the second women's liberation movement theatre has played a role of great significance, and it is vital that students of Feminism understand what the Women's Theatre companies of the 1970s stood for, both in terms of their effectiveness in making cultural change and in their contribution to individual transformation. The work of these companies, such as Monstrous Regiment and Siren was often tied with the women's conferences and events of that decade. The companies gave workshops as well as performances and from their work has grown the modern canon of women's theatre, both mainstream and experimental, and the work of the Feminist actors, directors, writers and stand up comics and cabaret artists who continue to create women's performance in many forms.

To understand the phenomenon of the contemporary Feminist theatre and to be able to contribute to it with their own work, students need to know the nature of male constructed female performance and grasp the relationship of this theatre to contemporary Feminist theory.

For this reason the course 'Women and Performance' takes a critical look at the male constructed performance of patriarchal culture. This study takes the form of describing the images, the dilemmas and the survivors. For the images we may look for example at the world of cinema and the idea of the female star. The students are encouraged to question the received images, to look at a range of stereotypes and to compare the public male constructed and perceived images of women with their own lived experience of explored reality.

Examples used in this discussion might include Marilyn Monroe, characters from Soap Opera and the images created for female pop and screen stars. The end of the century has brought its own new icons, the great classical actresses, such as Judi Dench and Juliet Stevenson and Janet MacAteer giving us their Feminist reconstructions of Hedda Gabler, Lady Macbeth and Mother Courage from the male canon, and directors such as Deborah Warner working at the Royal National Theatre and challenging traditional notions of the use of theatrical space as perceived by men. These women are not only working with new female identified insights and a clear sense of female identity in its own right, but also within the cultural elite, the class of people who go to live theatre, an ever dwindling group.

Perhaps more interesting in some ways are the Feminist reconstructions found in popular media and film. The discussion often includes the dilemmas for women created by the image projected by Madonna; to some a symbol of true liberation, to others a betrayal of Feminism and its ideals. It is also inclusive of the characters of powerful women portrayed by Jodie Foster in the *Silence of the Lambs* 1991, and Susan Sarandon in *Dead Man Walking* 1996, to take two examples from recent cinema, directed by men but centred on performance by women. There can be no doubt that these performances are influenced by Feminism, and the women who give them may be described as survivors of a conflict with the male creators. They are performing in the arena of popular culture, still largely in the male canon but in their own right as women, and bringing to that performance an understanding of the Female Performance that has been forged in a more experimental field, such as in the work of the companies of the 1970s and Magdalena project. The question central to these explorations is always 'Where does the male construct end and the woman's own self created image begin?'

Close to the Feminist ideal of performance, and yet in the popular arena, are those women who work from a lesbian perspective, for example the lesbian singer and actor k.d. lang. Her film *Salmonberries* 1993, is about a lesbian relationship but one that survives in a male dominated world of the frontierlands in the far North of the American continent. Similarly the recent *Serving in Silence*, a Television film about Marguerite Cammermeyer starring Glen Close, not only centred on a lesbian relationship but also portrayed the true story of Cammermeyer's defiance of the American laws excluding homosexuals from the armed forces, a struggle at the forefront of current Gay Liberation issues. This was shown on prime time television. Here was a performance concerning a woman not only surviving or reconstructing, but also actively engaged in struggle against the values of the most male dominated of all worlds.

The dilemmas for women in these forms of mainstream performance are about the lure of fame, recognition, success and money and the buying into the patriarchy as a norm to whatever extent. Of course these performers do Feminism a great and positive service by bringing women's issues into the mainstream arena and exploring the continuation of woman's oppression and how it is dealt with. However, they do not always give room to the possibility of a type of performance that is different in both form and essence to the male.

It is the possibility of a performance defined by the Feminist view and entirely different from male performance, that is supported by the French Feminist theorists, whose work is of central relevance to the course. Among these Helene Cixous is concerned with the ways in which a truly Feminist performance allows women to exit from being the symbols of male reality constructed by men. In her own play *The Portrait of Dora*, Cixous narrates the story of Dora exiting before diagnosis from the male psychological constructs of woman being laid on her by Sigmund Freud. Cixous suggests that in order to make this exit effective, women performers must try to construct their own symbols, and nowhere is this idea realised more beautifully and completely than in the work of Deborah Levy in her play *Heresies*, which provides a realisation of the fact that man has constructed woman as a symbol within his universe and woman must exit from this universe and create her own. Levy puts a man in the play as a visitor to the world of women in order to demonstrate how different that world is from his own which he has previously perceived as reality.

In Cixous' definition of female performance woman needed to be seen in her own right as strong, with the ability to generate energy and her own Feminist language. This idea is also explored by Dale Spender (1987) and in Mary Daly (1987) in their several theses on Feminist language. Above all else for Cixous the woman is the active protagonist of her reality and this idea clearly overturns the traditional male view of woman as the passive object of male action.

Another theorist, Luce Irigray is the critic of woman as negative, particularly in terms of sexual desire, definition and activity. Her theory is particularly concerned with woman's ownership of her own body an active, willing body, not a passive recipient of the male element. This concern has a very strong link with performance in that we are looking at the portrayal of women as sexual objects on films, pornography, prostitution. In the Feminist reconstruction of sex as performance we are looking at an emphasis on the physical aspects of theatre as in the work of a practitioner such as Anna Furse, and in the exploration of Lesbian sexuality as independent of the male as for example in the work of Lois Weaver and the growing canon of Lesbian experimental plays and films.

The third theorist is Julia Kristeva who is concerned with the world of communication, through words, and signs and symbols, with the semiotic of women's theatre, as opposed to the repression of women's semiotic by the male definition of all discourse. Her ideas have relevance to Feminist theatre chiefly in that women have been inspired by Kristeva to write in different constructs of time, not in the male construct of linearity, but using a cyclical model or different periods from the past in parallel. Examples of this are current in the mainstream work of Caryl Churchill. I have found that an acquaintance with the work of all these theorists is important to the student embarking on the practical experience of Feminist performance that the course seeks to provide.

The third crucial source is the growing canon of women's playwrighting and performance. For centuries women have watched performance of themselves within the male construct and the theatre has seemed entirely unreal to them and divorced from their reality and experience. The political work of the 1970s changed all that. For the first time women went to the theatre and heard and saw the narratives of their reality. They saw their oppression in comedy depicting their domestic roles in living with men. This was often done through cabaret acts at women's conferences, which provoked wild and joyous reactions. They saw the violence against them, and voiced their reactions in the work of SCUM (Society for Cutting up Men) and translated their anger into action in the work of WAVAW (Women Against Violence Against Women) both founded in Leeds.

Women began also to make theatre about the realities that are specific to women, childbirth, child care, women's health issues, menstruation and the menopause. Another whole strand of theatre dealt with the women together in the social context, in plays like Maureen Duffy's *Rites*, set in a ladies lavatory, and with the women's fears and treatment in the male world as in Louise Page's play *Tissu* which is about a woman who has a mastectomy.

The discovery and recovery of women's history become a pre occupation and both Sarah Daniels and Caryl Churchill wrote plays dealing with witch trials and linked them with modern reality. The common characteristic of all these works is that they are highly political, and present in righteous anger a coherent challenge to women's oppression. More recently the other taboos have been broken in plays like Sarah Daniels' *Masterpieces*, which is about snuff movies, and Eve Lewis' *Ficky Stingers*, which concerns date rape. Perhaps the most successful challenge made by women's theatre to patriachy has been to address the greatest taboo of all, the Lesbian realities and relationships. Lesbian comedy was once alternative cabaret, with group such as Sensible Footwear leading the field, and now it is in the mainstream with Hufty and Sandy Tocsvik appearing regularly on mainstream television and at live venues. From the 1970's work of Jill Posener and others in the 1970s we have arrived at the portrayal of Lesbians on the most popular soap operas. What has happened is that having moved out of the male reality to construct our own, we have moved back into it with our challenge.

Alongside mainstream and popular work was a growing body of experimental material, centred around the initiatives of the Magdalana project of 1986. This project sought to bring together women performers of many cultures and traditions, to share their work and define its commonalities and its distinctive characteristics. Out of this initiative has come a continuing research base for women's theatre and the work of companies like Freya in Denmark who host the bi-annual women's theatre festival. All this work responds to the need identified in women's theatre to tell the personal story and the empowerment that the recognition of that story brings. This strand of theatre is, if you like, the living proof that the personal is political.

The course and its teaching practice

To begin the section on practice I quote the title of a Lesbian play of the 1970s, Jill Posener's *Any Woman Can*. She was referring to choice of sexuality, but the phrase describes an approach to the students beginning a course in Feminist theatre, never having done any Drama before and claiming that they cannot act, draw, sing, dance or write and that they do not have any imagination. These claims are a measure to me both of the low self esteem with which many women are still conditioned to approach a new experience and of the general cultural view that creativity is for the elite few, which the consensus of society, usually male society, agrees are artists.

Dorothy Heathcote through her work in creating Drama in education, pronounces that Drama is a basic human need, and that without the opportunities that Drama offers to reflect on our lives and society, we are not able to function as fully operative human beings (Wagner, 1976). The facilitator of Drama workshops has to approach them with the unshakeable belief that any woman can invent and take part in a piece of theatre at whatever is her level of ability. All she needs is the will and the opportunity which the course hopes to be able to provide.

In the workshop sessions of the course I work through the process of creating images, creating dialogue or monologue and then moving on to create the dramatic structures of character and situation to underpin them. These are the basic skills common to almost any course in acting. But before any of this can happen, the members of the group have to generate the material. The first consideration here is that it is not possible to make or perform Drama about any topic unless there is an emotional engagement. The first part of the process therefore is to identify those topics with which the several members of the group have a common emotional engagement. This process in itself requires trust and a sense of group membership and dynamic. No-one is going to reveal their feelings, or anything of their inner life to other people whom they do not know and trust. The first sessions of theory and image making generate both the material and the group dynamic. What happens is that the members of the group discover common interests, attitudes and experiences. Starting with straightforward discussion techniques and moving on to create simple images sets in motion a wellspring of creativity in which the members of the group realise their inner creative selves and share them with each other.

The techniques of image making are taken from the work of Augusto Boal (1978) and include simple human sculptures and the discovery through image making of the power of the body to express beyond words. The images made will respond to a simple idea offered by the facilitator or by one of the group. The images are seen by the other members of the group, and commented on and described, and gradually the significance goes beyond that which we originally intended. These techniques are widely tried and tested in contemporary theatre practice, particularly in areas where a pedagogical approach is needed. They never fail to amaze those who create them, astounded at the release of the creative and imaginative power, that they had so vehemently denied. What emerges from the image making is a collection of ideas, all of which are noted though as yet they are not structured into any particular form. Unknown to the participants there also emerges the beginning of performance skill.

From this image making the next task is to create dialogue and monologue, words with which the images may be further explained and explored. A useful technique for this is one I came across in the work of Gay Sweatshop, known as impulse writing. The purpose of this is to try to reach behind the normal inhibitions of ordinary life and create language from impulse. The individual is invited to write privately starting with given phrase and without pausing for several minutes. If the flow breaks, the writer had to start again from the beginning, This private writing is then practised several times and then edited before being shared by the group. If the writing is based on material drawn from the images, what emerges is a range of linguistic interpretations and commentaries on those images, which further develops and informs the work. At this point it is possible to introduce more conventional theatre structures and skills, creating and developing character and situation, using the techniques developed by Stanislavski which create emotional engagement, and editing the written material further into dialogue or monologue as appropriate. By this time the original images are completely transformed and something very like a performance is beginning to emerge.

To this material we can add objects to use as symbols and to generate metaphors. Using objects is the simplest way of accessing symbolic meaning, whether we are using a photograph to represent a relationship, or natural objects to communicate more abstract meaning. The precedent for this approach lies in the work of the Magdalena project in 1986. Here a number of performers, coming from other countries and cultures, introduced women from Europe to the idea of performance using physical work, voice, environment and objects. This was a way of creating an alternative to the traditional in Eurocentric and United States theatre, of the realist linear narrative or the epic or expressionist traditions all of which were dominated by male practitioners and writers. At this stage the group are usually well on the way to creating their own performance piece and the time has come for the facilitator to take a step back from the process to reflect and notice what is happening and begin to make her analysis.

The Analysis

In the last two years of delivering the course I have noticed two strands of material emerging at this final stage. One I call the personal story and the other I call the staging of stereotypes. The women who created the Magdalena project noticed the first strand, of personal stories, emerging as integral to women's performance work. These narratives were based on an individual experience but once they are made into performance they become the shared and recognised experience in the first instance of the group, and in the second of their audience. The element of recognition of women's common experience is of particular significance. The personal stories emerge to contribute to the creative material of the course and in their emergence the tellers find recognition from the other members of the group. Alongside the personal stories, and often interwoven with them, comes the consciousness raising, the stories of learning and transformation which describe the ways in which an awareness of Feminism has been life transforming for the individuals concerned.

In the context of the course these personal stories are subsumed, as the piece moves towards performance, into a series of critical presentations of stereotypes. What fascinates me is that from two completely different groups of students who knew nothing about each other's work, roughly the same groups of stereotypes have emerged in performance. The element in common has been that both times the course has run we have used the same two play texts, Deborah Levy's *Pax* and Eve Lewis's *Ficky Stingers*. The first of these plays is concerned with archetypal female figures which create and operate in their own universe. The second, mentioned above, is a violent and realistic Drama about date rape.

The stereotypes that emerged from the devising process were called into question and examined critically in the performance. Some stereotypes were present in both year groups of students on the course, among them the single mother, the upper class rich bored and unhappy woman, the working-class woman as caricature char lady, and the rape survivor. Those who emerged only in one year were the career woman and the prostitute. There were other characters who were more individualised, but the structure and pace of the pieces depended on the use of the stereotypes as central.

In my reflection on the emergence of these stereotypes the following questions become important. 'Why did stereotypes emerge at all?' and 'Why these particular ones?', and perhaps more significantly 'What semiotic communication did they make with the audience?' and 'What was intended by the actors?'

The answer to the first question demonstrates that stereotypes can also be archetypes with elements of truth, even if that truth has become caricature. The truth of them is expressed both in audience recognition and laughter and in the actors' creation of them from their own experience. Some of the students found playing these characters immensely liberating. They enjoyed exaggerating the characteristics within themselves and externalising part of their own personality that they might otherwise have wished to conceal. In the case of the comedy characters, such as the char ladies, the work was, I suspect, motivated by a desire to get an audience to laugh with you as a caricature, rather than at you because of your working-class accent and attitudes in a largely middle class institution. It was also clear in some of the portrayals that there was an element of recognition on the part of the actor of an aspect of herself that she did not particularly like, maybe the snob or the eternal complainer. These aspects of an individual can be externalised and acknowledged without the actor feeling that anyone thinks that

that is what she is really like. These two characteristics seem to suggest that the playing of these stereotypes were in part at least, therapeutic or cathartic in that it enabled individuals to look at, and to some extent deal with aspects of themselves and their lives that were problematic. This was borne out in the material presented in the students' note-books and in their evaluations.

The stereotypes were also played both for sympathy and for criticism. In the case of the career woman and upper-class bored and unhappy woman, the responses that the actors wished to draw from the audience were a mixture of both. It was assumed that the audience would react to these stereotypes critically. The performances attempted to turn expectations on their heads and to present a more sympathetic side to characters who at first seemed unbelievable. In the case of the rape survivor and the single parent, these characters may have been criticised or misunderstood on the stage, through the portrayal of their treatment by men, but the audience was meant to feel sympathy for them. There was a subtlety of approach to the presentation of these characters who clearly challenged the male constructs of them and created a Feminist dialectic.

Some of these stereotypical characters were entirely positive, powerful figures, women whose virtues of kindness and gentleness, humour and wisdom, and whose ability to survive suffering, and to be positively angry, were their great strengths. These characters were often based on those of Deborah Levy, and through creating them in improvisation, the students gave expression to the positive, spiritual and poetic aspects of women's theatre and in their own way contributed towards the creation of a Female Performance.

In both this and the political aspects of the course, I believe that students are helped to understand the empowering potential of Women's Studies in the form of theatre. Women's Theatre enables us to learn from other women, from their experience, their artistic work and their culture and identity. Above all through the study and experience of performance in Women's Studies women come to believe in their creative selves and in their ability both to make, and eventually change, reality in their own definitions.

9 Reflections of a Black woman reflecting

Philomena Carlotta Hilaria Harrison

> How can we separate our race from our sex, our sex from our race? And we hear again and again we must struggle against sexism at the exclusion of racism. To remain private with change is to self-destruct; to go public with change is to begin to challenge the forces of white supremacy.
>
> - excerpts from *Under Our Own Wings*, Nellie Wong (Featherston,1994, p.71).

Task: Using a novel or other text written by a woman, reflect upon the impact it has made on your personal development.

For me, at that point in my life the choice came very easily. I even became excited at the prospect of writing such an essay! My choice of text to complete the course work was related to my own personal development; my functioning as a Black woman in both the private and public spheres. The text I chose at that time was *Sisters of the Yam*, (bell hooks, 1993). *Into the Melting Pot* has provided me with the opportunity to reflect further on that experience and its relevance to the teaching of Women's Studies. How can we teach or learn with understanding if we have not explored our own lives and tried to make sense of that experience; tried to understand the relevance of our personal biographies with any degree of honesty.

Before speaking to a group of (mostly female and all White) students about Black Feminisms I felt compelled to tell them a little about my story, why I might be offering them a particular perspective. My experience in teaching and training on issues around oppression has convinced me that this process is important for both teachers and learners, particularly so for courses such as Women's Studies and Social Work. Given that the participants will come to their learning with diverse backgrounds and life experiences it is crucial for them to be aware of how those experiences influence their learning. All of us engaged in the process of learning need to come to a level of awareness that makes us conscious of what

drives the processing of information and the search for new knowledge. Why we might reject certain texts, information or lectures! bell hooks takes up Paulo Freire's view of education as offering opportunities for the practice of freedom.
'I entered the classrooms with the conviction that it was crucial for me and every other student to be an active participant and not a passive consumer.' (hooks, 1994, p.15) and 'When education is the practice of freedom, students are not the only ones who are asked to share, confess. Engaged pedagogy does not seek simply to empower students. Any classroom that employs a holistic model of learning will also be a place where teachers grow, and are empowered by the process.' (hooks, 1994, p.21).

To bring any notion of empowerment to the learning situation we need to take risks in what we share. I take this risk again and wish to share some of my story with you. It is a little of my story till now. It will chart and reflect on my life experience in a white supremist, patriarchal world. Its approach is 'routed' in Black Feminism. In many ways it reflects the notion of a 'melting pot', yet I hope retains my individuality.

Theorising by Black Feminists is rooted in the exploration and the telling of those life stories (Brewer, 1994, James and Busia, 1994, p.15). Telling it in a way that is both honest and accessible. In recent years we have begun to have more access to the writings of women in the Southern and Northern worlds; Black, Asian, Chinese and women of diverse backgrounds, colour and culture are theorising and writing about the nature of their lives. Through their novels, autobiographies, essays and poetry they have challenged racism, sexism and homophobia, despite the fact that society remains white, male and heterosexually dominated.

The work of these women has forced us to look at the way in which systems of domination interconnect and oppress the individual. Central to Black Feminist thinking and theorising is the notion of the 'simultaneity of oppression' (Brewer quoting Hull et al. in James and Busia, p.16). With reference to the Clarence Thomas v Anita Hill case, what weighting did the white women, who came to her support, give to Anita Hill's race? Was their support guided by the commonality of gender? Or was that society merely protecting the masculinity of Clarence Thomas? Through such public events, and the continuing 'everyday racism' (Essed, 1991, p.vii) and sexism, Black women have realised that the struggle continues. Through the writings and actions of many Black women and women of colour, Black women are moving, on an individual and collective level, to no longer being 'de mule uh de world ' (Neal Hurston, 1937, p.29).

The struggle then is at both the individual and societal level. The Black woman's struggle is not merely against the forces of any one single oppression, but the combined forces of oppression existing for the many social divisions to which an individual may belong (race, gender, sexual orientation, disability).

I have been moved by the writings of many Black women - poets, intellectuals, novelists, letters and cards from friends - during the past ten years of my life. hooks' text came at a timely moment. It confirmed some changes I had already made in my life, affirmed parts that were already me, and gave me knowledge and understanding to continue in that process; changes I have naturally incorporated into my working and personal life. I have become clearer about my direction, my limitations and the need for collective struggle. My story and my recent experiences makes me need to say that I have taken some White women and men with me on my journey. That involvement, as with my Black friends and family, has been one of joy, expectations, insecurity, disappointments, sharing, loss and much love.

> Trapped in a world of my own making?
> Thinking, forever creating
> A way out of the web
> Of love, commitment, guilt
> To move through and into
> An identity all my own.
> (Philomena Harrison, unpublished)

The Black Lesbian Feminist writer Audre Lorde has written many moving essays and poetry. bell hooks was inspired by her writing, living and teaching. She quotes the following from Lorde's essay 'Eye to eye'. (in hooks, 1993, p.6).

> Learning to love ourselves as Black women goes beyond a simplistic insistence that "Black is Beautiful". It goes beyond and deeper than the surface appreciation of Black beauty, although that is certainly a good beginning. But if the quest to reclaim ourselves and each other remains there, then we accept another superficial measurement of self, one superimposed upon the old one and almost as damaging, since it pauses at the superficial. Certainly it is no more empowering. And it is empowerment - our strengthening in the service of ourselves and each other, in the service of our work and future - that will be the result of this pursuit.

The coming together of Black women in sisterhood is part of the process of change. Part of that process is the need to come to love ourselves through the action of that reclamation of self. Though the achievement of awareness brings us joy, the struggles continue. I felt very much a part of the latter view expressed by hooks in the text, as I engaged, and continue to do so, in those changes. From my own life and that of the many Black and White working class women with whom I have worked, is that even in the midst of struggle women can engage in and understand that wider political context of their experience. What they may not have (at any particular point in time) is the energy to effect change. The impact of racism and sexism is draining. No assumptions can be made about their understanding or longing to engage in that wider struggle.

In an oppressive world, women need that support to engage in the process of change. bell hooks' book has spoken to me and allowed me to continue in that change and the route to self-recovery. 'Sisters of the Yam' was originally a self-help and support group formed by hooks in response to the needs of her Black female students who were doing Women's Studies (specifically Black Women's Studies), studying works of Toni Morrison, Paula Marshal, Alice Walker, Audre Lorde. They came to hooks to 'confess the truth of their lives'. Like many of the characters in the novels, these students' lives were influenced by rape, violence, incest. They had low self-esteem, they were attempting suicide. Though these students were from privileged backgrounds they were suffering the same psychological problems as those Black people in poverty - problems that are generally explained merely in economic terms without looking at the interconnectedness of aspects of peoples' lives. In and through the groups Black women examined the factors in their lives which would lead to hurt and pain; the structures of domination that continue to disadvantage the Black woman: racism, sexism, homophobia, poverty, disability, class. My work experience, and existing research, in this country has told me that in the treatment of their mental distress Black women are more likely to receive medication and less likely to be offered appropriate counselling or psychotherapy (Ismail K. in Abel K., et al 1996, pp.69, 76). The dimensions of race, class and other relevant social divisions need to be constantly there in any analyses., whether for assessment or treatment.

hooks sees the power of healing as one that should come out of the 'community and communion with Black people'. She feels we should draw on the traditional ways of living; conversation, story telling, drawing on the spiritual dimensions of our lives. *Sisters of the Yam* is seen as a way of that journey to self-recovery.
hooks ends the first chapter by quoting a student seeking recovery: 'Healing occurs through testimony, through gathering together everything available to you and reconciling.' (hooks, 1993, p.17).

To write further I too need to 'gather together', to chart my story. In that process I hope also to address some points of healing: emphasising again, the centrality of biography in the theorising of Black Feminisms; that location in time and place, linking the personal and political.

My life began in Calcutta, India. I am the third child of a family of seven surviving children; the eighth (fifth born) died around the age of two of complications following whooping cough. I wonder now how much space the nature of my mother's life gave her to grieve. I have four sisters and two brothers. My birth is recorded as 'a female child born to Sri G.B.Williams'. No name, no mother! I received my 'Christian name' when I was baptised into the Roman Catholic church. It is my baptism certificate that my insurers in this country find more acceptable. I keep them both safely, together; they say a lot about who I am.

My parents were both born and brought up in India, their life experience being dominated by the Raj, and British Empire. I see myself very much as a product, biologically and psychologically, of that Empire. As a Black woman I have seen myself as a Victim of that Empire.

The origins of my father lie in slavery and colonialism. His father, Algernon

Alexander Williams, was born on the island of St Vincent (a group of islands referred to as St Vincent and the Grenadines), in 1876 to parents whose immediate ancestors were brought as slaves from Africa to that part of the world to work on the sugar plantations. I was very moved to see a picture of my great, great grandmother. The image was very much that of the one I had built up through my life of what this 'breed of people called slaves' were like; passive, but I saw a strength. It is important to understand and know the sources of these images to make any sense at all of the impact of internalised racism. When I recently visited the island, people kept asking me are you a Vincentian? I wanted desperately to say 'Yes, I am'. Instead, I offered 'My grandfather was born here'. They responded 'Well then, you are a Vincentian'. For those beautiful moments I 'belonged'. But it was more than that. It was my concrete link with slavery, empire, oppression, racism. The plantation house, now a hotel, told me that. It was there in the faces and the eyes of the Black people who worked there; those of mixed parentage, and lighter skins, having the administrative jobs. I know that my grandfather travelled on merchant ships as a ships engineer; I have his disembarking papers. Finally, at the age of twenty three, he settled in Calcutta. Here he married my grandmother and they subsequently had 6 children; my father, George Betram Williams, being one of two surviving males.

My mother's parents were linked with colonialism in a different way. Her mother, Lucy Butcher was born in India and saw herself as Goan (of Portuguese and Indian parentage); her mother, Florence D'Santos being Goan and her father a British soldier. My mother's father was English and came from Rochdale. He was there in Calcutta as an employee of Burmah Shell. So my mother grew up as a member of a minority group referred to as Anglo Indians. My childhood memory tells me that they despised and were despised by the general Indian population. The Anglo Indians fashioned their lives very much on the style of the English in India. Most people lived out their lives in that way, waiting for the time when they could (as my family did) return to the 'mother country'. Aspects of that existence are well portrayed in Paul Scott's novel *Staying On* (Scott P.1977).

The culture then of my upbringing was essentially British/English. I attended a Church of England boarding school from the age of four to fifteen years. Though students who boarded had to be Christians, the day students came from a range of Indian cultures and religions. About twenty percent of the student group were Chinese.

It was here in the Welland Goldsmith School I read Enid Blyton, golliwogs and all! English and European History was a core area of learning. Indian history charted the various viceroys of India; ending with Mountbatten. The learning of mathematics included being competent in the use of British currency (pounds, shillings and pence). English literature was the only literature. All students had to learn two Indian languages; Hindi and Bengali. Father Christmas came for everyone - in a rickshaw usually.

Contradicting the expectations of most women in Indian society at that time, praise was for those most academically able. The typing pool and the domestic class were shunned. The majority of the Anglo-Indian young people in my school (mostly working class) did not achieve well academically. They were not expected to. This added to their feelings of confusion in relation to notions of superiority over Indians. This, I feel, confused and compounded their marginalised position in that society.

It was in this arena that I learned quickly about my difference. The development then of my racial identity, because of the impact of colonialism, was fraught with doubts and some measure of confusion in the world outside my family. My curly hair, and my father's clear non-Indian features affirmed my difference. What I grew up with was having to match up and make sense of what was happening in the public and private spheres of my life. Out there I was a negro, a 'nigger'; my father was there to prove it, the text books said so too.

I achieved well academically. I escaped the domestic class and the typing pool! My family came to England, to Liverpool, to Liverpool 8, in 1966. The green and pleasant land was not all we thought it to be. It was then I began my real understanding and experience of what racism was, and the impact it would have on my life. I spent a year in a local secondary modern school and at sixteen years of age began my working life. Not a matter of choice, but necessity, as my parents' income did not allow the luxury of further study of a family member who was capable of self sufficiency. I came some twenty years later to higher education, social work and lecturing.

During my developing years, my father, through a pride I knew not the source of, gave me a very positive image of myself. He talked to me of his ancestors and mine. They were African chiefs, a proud people; and that I was beautiful, clever and strong, and was never to believe anything different. Was this the story telling tradition coming through my father's ancestors? My mother always confirmed these ideas, while at the same time preparing me to deal with the effects of racism, even in Indian society. Black Feminist thought in its development and theorising is anchored in the telling of stories, telling those life experiences and making sense of them. hooks suggests that that process is the route to self-recovery. (hooks, 1993, p.19).

In making these reflections I posed the question to myself, 'Is there no self-recovery where there is no history, no story to tell? For people of the African diaspora, particularly so for those of mixed parentage, holding on to those stories is no easy task. The Indian government has denied me my Indian nationality; because my parents held British passports at the time of my birth.

In the process of looking to my points of healing I discovered that I was given a story from both my parents. The impact of internalised racism has made me, for so many years, forget what they gave me. I always saw those stories merely as something to bolster me through the years of being bombarded with negative images of Black people; particularly those of African origin.

My practice as social worker and my work with Black students has demonstrated that for women to achieve any sense of recovery/healing or maximise their learning, they need to assess and understand the impact of race and gender (and other social divisions to which they may belong) on their lives. It is important :

> ... to understand that "the experience of being woman can create an illusionary unity, for it is not the experience of being woman, but the meanings attached to gender, race, class and age at various historical moments" (p.86), that it is important to grasp. Hence the need to "locate the politics of experience" (Mohanty in Lewis, 1996, p.27).

I move now to hooks' first point of healing - that of truth telling. (hooks,1993, p.19). It is a commitment to telling that truth that is the first step in the process of healing. To get to know ourselves we need to accept certain truths about ourselves. The dehumanising of African slaves and the success of that slavery would not have been possible without the wholesale deceit of many people. Those myths were there in my developing years and had a deep impact on my psyche. I have had to look back with honesty at those times of longing to deny my colour, to be something other than that defined 'Other'. The negro slave had to hide behind a wall of deceit and lies in order to survive - to escape the brutality of the master. But we need to, with truth and honesty, name our oppression.

How safe then is truth telling in a society where racism is endemic? What strategies do we use in preparing our children to deal with the realities of the experience of racism? I have a personal philosophy of generally speaking the truth about my life including in the professional sphere. My growing awareness and observations of the nature of both racism and sexism in organisations makes me question the limits of 'telling it as it is' - to rethink the impact of 'telling' on my professional standing. Psychologically, this is a struggle, as it equates to lying to myself. This is certainly an area of stress for me, because it brings me full circle to hooks' thinking about Black folks having to lie to survive in a White supremist patriarchal society. How far in truth telling do we risk confirming the stereotypes of Black women and Black families?

Truth telling is not a simple process, but yet it is a necessary part of healing. If we are able to limit denial in our lives we may then be able also to shake off the shackles of racism and reduce its dysfunctioning impact on our lives. That truth telling becomes liberating.

How we see ourselves, in the context of a White society, has an effect on our self concept and identity as Black women. Traditionally, Blackness has been defined for us by White people. I grew up surrounded by many of these negative notions. They were confirmed in social relationships outside of my family through the media and literature. Where do we find access to positive images of Black femaleness? It is not enough to know or hear that black is beautiful. In examining the process, the history of how those negative images appear and are sustained, Black women (Black people) have come to know where these changes need to be made.

hooks cites an excellent example, affecting most Black women of African origin. How and where do we learn that our hair is a problem? I recall, with pain, my early childhood experiences in relation to hair - my hair. It defined me as a negro - an inferior. The shouts of 'curly tops' ring out loud and clear. To feel 'the same' you long to be rid of what marks you as apart from others. In school my hair was seen as a problem - to be cut off. This has been, until recently, the experience of many Black children in the care system in this country. Straight, flowing hair is seen as being easier to manage and sexually more attractive. These images still remain, even in magazines for Black women. hooks discusses the view that it could have been at one time that the nature of Black women's lives made it helpful to have straight hair that was quicker to manage. When such a situation might no longer exist why do such views and actions still exist? Is straight hair now a fashion? Styling and hair care has been and still is an important part of African society; indicating beauty and status. At the age of forty I left my long hair (my 'curly tops') open for the first time in my life. The compliments stay with me. My hair felt powerful - I felt good!

Skin colour is another area that cannot go unaddressed in looking to healing and self worth. While negative images of Blackness are embedded in White culture the task of helping children conceive of themselves under the umbrella of 'Black' is a difficult one. Especially when a child is faced daily with 'black' being a term of abuse. This has been the case for young children with whom I have worked on issues of racial identity. My work with them helps them to chart their stories, and explore the goodness. Children are exposed to racism in their peer groups, and in the education system. As Black women and mothers, hooks suggests we need to examine our own 'deep seated' feelings and ideas about hair or skin colour and look closely at what negative images we might be unwittingly communicating to our children. I would add that we need to look at ways in which we as mothers/parents can engage actively in the process of education, so that the positive images children may get in the closeness of their families are not negated in the other social systems to which they are exposed. But firstly, we need to learn to love our Blackness in its entirety; to love ourselves because of ourselves, not despite ourselves.

Understanding and knowing about ourselves at work was an important point of healing for hooks. Black women have always worked - in the home, in other people's homes, in the fields and industry. Racism has for many Black women defined the jobs they have traditionally occupied. Work may often be seen as a means to an end; the way to earn money to live and survive. To make work 'sweet' we need to experience a certain quality of work. hooks sees this process as being able to make choices in the work that we do. This relates to the notion of 'right livelihood', coming out of Buddhist writing on the subject (hooks, 1993, p.46).

Is this journey accessible to all Black women? I think not. The converging forces of the oppressions of race, gender, class and poverty will render many Black women powerless to make changes. For those who do, the journey can be one fraught with pain, and the need for constant vigilance. As Black women in any place of work we need to be aware of the roles that we assume. How often are they the ones that are related to 'servicing'? As a Black tutor I have needed to be aware of what I am able to do in the support of Black students and colleagues. Does that role quickly become my personal responsibility? At what point does the organisation opt out of its responsibilities? As a Black women I must have strategies to manage these situations if work is to be kept 'sweet'. The way forward has been to use the support of Black women colleagues, Black friends, my sisters and white colleagues who have moved some way along the road to understanding the deeper issues in the web of racism and sexism.

The challenges have to be made again and again, in public, and not alone. As a Black lecturer and trainer I have many opportunities to promote the principles of anti-oppressive practice (its origins in Black Feminist thought). I have opportunities to ask white groups of students and social workers, how many times recently had they had to think about, examine, explain or account for their whiteness, and as they shake their heads and smile their 'noes', I can tell them that as a Black woman I have to do that every day of my life. My story, may help them understand why.

Healing and self recovery needs to address the nature of love, giving and loss. hooks looks at the experience of Black people loving in and through the experience of slavery and racism. The conditions that existed in slavery, and today the effects of apartheid in South Africa has made it very difficult for Black people to love with confidence. The constant nature of change and loss in people's lives can make loving a frustrating experience. If racism does not allow you to love yourself, how do you learn to love others? The impact of loss, inhibits our capacity to love. I felt this recently at the death of a close female friend. I felt afraid to get close to anyone else, to avoid that pain. Black people, like others living in an oppressive society, have had to adopt repression as a defence mechanism for survival. But: 'When we love ourselves, we know that we must do more than survive. We must have the means to live fully. To live fully, Black women can no longer deny our need to know love.' (hooks, 1993, p.137).

Through sexism and racism Black women have been socialised into being givers and carers, giving of ourselves to children, men, work. Does our love become a commodity, like our sexuality? In being able to love appropriately we need to be able to respond to our own emotional needs, moving from denial to acceptance of those needs. We are not responsible for doing all the loving - being the ever constant providers. We can love ourselves and be loved for what or who we are. It takes time to learn that you are loveable for yourself, not for what you have given or are capable of giving. My children challenge me, painfully, but yet demand my love. If I did not know that I was loved by them and others, and gave love, I would be broken. Looking at love helps us focus on our own emotional needs. hooks sees this as a positive approach because it shifts the focus from us merely trying to meet material needs.

Alongside loving we need to look to spirituality in our lives. For some it is attained through religious beliefs. hooks advises in her text that to move out of the stress of our everyday existence and experiences we need solitude as part of the healing process. We all need and long for a place described by the mysterious voice in Toni Morrison's novel *Jazz*.

> I want to be in a place already made for me, both snug and wide open. With a doorway never needing to be closed, a view slanted for light and bright autumn leaves but not rain. Where moonlight can be counted on if the sky is clear and stars no matter what
> (Morrison, 1992, p.221).

hooks' analysis provides the reader with individual solutions. It nevertheless puts the process and the experience of self-recovery and healing in a social and political context; examining the effect of theorising, and practice on the functioning of the individual. By adding my stories I have tried to mirror that process.

My own capacity to occupy more than one social and racial (acknowledging the problems and discourse in respect of using the term race) position has driven me to explore and try to explain the issues around my developing Black womanhood, the nature of my identity. I observe other Black women in this society and ask how their ideas would fit with mine. We all experience racism. How and where have their subjectivities developed? Many other Black women and women of colour, will have stories to tell; our stories connect, yet can be so different. You may learn from them, but first you need to be able to tell your story.

Reading *Sisters of the Yam* took me to points of healing on my map of self-recovery; one which was important to undertake because of the impact of racism and sexism in my life. It is important to say that many of these points of healing and the nature of oppression relate to many of the other social divisions in which people may find themselves; including Black women. I would not wish to devalue or negate the impact of oppression on the lives of those people whilst examining my own. I have drawn briefly on my history and life experience to examine my Blackness and womanhood. What then has come out of this Melting Pot?

I have begun to set free the Black woman in me.

10 Agenda for Women's Studies in the context of cultural diversity issues

Sneh Shah

Women's Studies for the new millennium need to be amended in the light of debates surrounding cultural diversity issues. The revision should reflect the cultural diversity in our British and global societies and cater for the needs of the different ethnic groups. Women's Movements have generally been based on revisiting the past, revealing women's values and contributions. The debates about cultural diversity have also looked at the past, but more from the point of understanding how it has shaped present inequalities.

An agenda for Women's Studies for the year 2000 has to be dictated by the aim of empowering all women and enabling them to work together while maintaining their individual and cultural identities. Within this context there is much to be gained by Women's Studies from analysing key facets of cultural diversity debates in Britain. This will focus on movements and debates, Women's Studies will be able to use this emphasis on change to become a more enabling academic study. This is particularly important, as has been clearly stated by Lynne Segal in 'Ten Years' After', in *Every Women*, March 1995, no. 2, p. 15. '... the spread of Women's Studies produced a growing academicisation of feminist theory. Such concepts had little in common with the confident sense of shared "sisterhood" once propelling women into militant defiance.'

Current focus on cultural diversity of women's issues

The raising of women's issues has, until the 1970s, been primarily done by white middle-class women. The movement was based very much within the framework of existing British society. Women's issues began to have implications for wider society with the concern about female under-representation in certain skills. For instance, with the 1970s, Education Departments started focusing on the role of schools in combating the gender imbalance in occupations such as engineering and science. Overall, the term 'equal opportunities' sums up the focus of women's issues in Britain: parity with men by way of the same opportunities for jobs. The debates emphasised rights but only had limited focus on the structural inequalities and fundamental changes needed in established structures to bring about change.

As a national mover, the women's issues lobby has been reasonably successful. However, as stated by Lynne Segal: 'It's not so much that feminism in the 1980s lost its way. It is rather that it has travelled in so many different directions that now its trajectories neither intersect, nor reflect the sentiments which once inspired women.'

Much more serious, however, was the relationship between the British White Women's movements and minority ethnic groups. Lynne Segal's words are again relevant: 'Many different forces were involved in the fragmentation of feminism during the 1980s. Conflicts between feminists became more hostile as we faced the hierarchical divisions between women along the lines of race, ethnicity, class, age, disability, or religion ...'

Doreen Cameron, then President of NATFHE, writing in the same issue of *Every Women* is more forthright:

> One of the failures of the women's movement has been the unwillingness to focus more directly on changes which directly affect Black Women, or women with disabilities. This failure to connect sufficiently with race, class and age does a real disservice to all women, but cannot endure a system which treats some of our sisters better and ignores the demands of others.

The women's movements in Britain took place in the racist context of society and when put side by side, racism in White women was generally stronger than the spirit of sisterhood. A few non-White women, generally from professional backgrounds, were attracted to women's movements, but the majority were much more conscious of the debilitating effect of racism on their own condition and circumstances. This feeling of sisterhood for many of the non-White women, was applicable only to other non-White women, and anger and frustration was directed against the whole of White society, including White women.

Over the past few years, however, there has been a growing consciousness of similarities in the challenges to anti-racism and anti-sexism, and readiness to work together. A call to merge the Commission of Racial Equality and the Equal Opportunities Commission has been one example. However, separate focus on individual causes such as racism, and gender inequality is seen to be necessary by groups, while not precluding co-operation with one another.

Relevant aspects of the cultural diversity developments

The following points have been selected as indicators for widening the scope for Women's Studies as an enabling curriculum. These are: different models of culturally diverse societies and their implications; racism, prejudice and race relations; perceptions of people from different cultural backgrounds; definitions and ownerships of agendas; relationships of minority ethnic women and men; and gender consciousness and minority ethnic women's groups.

Different models and culturally diverse society

The assimilation model

Newcomers to society could be expected, through specific policy, or as a result of the lack of specific provision for them, to become a part of the majority society and lose their identity and separateness. An assimilationist model puts emphasis for change on the newcomers. There could, sometimes, be grudging acknowledgement that the outsiders exist. A good example is given by Richardson (1994, pp.5-6) in *New Era in Education* where he refers to a poem by Shahida Janjua, *Tourism*. The poem begins with an evocation of exoticism:

> I was a caged animal
> Again today
> Stalked, trapped
> Put on display
> In the zoo
> They so graciously call
> An Ethnic Minority Community

An absorption into the main institutions of society by the newcomers is accompanied by freedom to continue operating in their individual and traditional cultural/social frameworks. This is the most widespread result in culturally diverse societies such as Britain.

Cultural pluralism

This approach on the other hand, focuses on the virtually separate existence of ethnic groups. In many respects, while the term has been widely used, its vagueness is an indicator of how muddled the thinking about different terms has been.

American sociologists had focused on a more comprehensive result of different cultures living together but which has not been widely considered in Britain; while the melting-pot theory has now been abandoned, its legacy indicates that the existence of different cultures could mean some changes for the majority as well as the minority cultures. In Britain, the focus on the values and positions of minority cultures has been a catalyst for a reactionary approach, leading to an elevation of traditional British culture and values.

Racism, prejudice and race relations

A focus on multi-culturalism and cultural diversity did not acknowledge the significance of racism in the attitudes of both minority and majority cultures, and in power relations. The recent official emphasis in Britain on more assimilationist policies has been based on more right wing racism, backed up by legislation. The historical contribution of different cultural groups in Britain has been significant. Yet in recent decades the race card has been very influential in politics.

Perceptions of people from different cultural backgrounds

Images are built up of people, often based on unconscious socialisation, but with very strong and deep-rooted results. There have been contradictions in cultural diversity issues: on the one hand, much work has been directed at counterbalancing racial and cultural stereotypes in people's minds; while on the other, new stereotypes, often equally unrealistic, have been created. The interpretation in Britain has excluded the majority as an ethnic group. Philosophies around culture can be accused of creating more divisions than understanding. A multi-ethnic approach highlights the separateness of groups in a culturally diverse society. The celebration of diversity in this context generally takes the form of the attractiveness of the exotic, like sarees, samosas and steel bands. Celebration of cultures in this way can distract from the fact that cultures are NOT static, and individuals are generally likely to have multiple cultural loyalties. There is again, no reference to any real change in society but the new cultural groups are a little like novelties in a zoo.

Richardson refers to white views of black and ethnic minority people being dehumanising not only for the oppressed but also for the oppressors. Janjua continues:

> So you learnt nothing
> Stuck with pre-conceptions
> Stuck with stereotypes
> You went and returned
> With post-car images
> Cardboard cut-out puppets
> Fleshless, Loveless, contact

Which leaves you
With more to worry about
Than me

Ethnic monitoring has been widely debated over the past few decades, and the wider agreement has been that the true nature and extent of disadvantage suffered by minority ethnic communities can only become clear if there is ethnic monitoring. Different categories have been used, such as in the 1991 population census. This has helped in clearing some adverse myths about minorities and immigrants, but it has also helped in the continuance of much stereotyping.

Definitions of ownerships of agendas

One of the most noticeable aspects of developments in the field of cultural diversity in Britain has been the lack of involvement by significant numbers of people and groups from minority ethnic backgrounds, and sometimes hostility to the official policies. A multicultural education industry grew up and created an agenda. It was Maureen Stone (1981) who drew attention to the misguidedness of some of the policies and assumptions and referred to what many of the minority ethnic communities themselves wanted. Her approach was criticised by many multicultural education experts, but more attention to Stone's thesis would have highlighted that the wishes and bypassing of the many minority ethnic people were ignored, causing hostility.

There was a focus in much of the literature on the voices of the minority ethnic communities themselves being heard, but academics and educationalists, who had the advantage of being a part of the established structures, provided the parameters. Many minority ethnic individuals accepted this as being one of the very few venues for expression.

Relationships of minority ethnic women and men

White women's movements in Britain have bypassed racism. For the majority of minority ethnic communities, the priority has been racism. Wallace (1979, p.13) highlights one aspect of Black women's relationships that has been overlooked in the multicultural debates:

> ... For perhaps the last fifty years there has been a growing distrust, even hatred, between black men and black women. It has been nursed along not only by racism on the part of the whites but also by an almost deliberate ignorance on the part of blacks about the sexual politics of their experience in this country.

Black women would often be torn between fighting against racism, and fighting for their own positions against Black men.

Gender consciousness and minority ethnic women's groups

Within Feminism, White women could only talk about the disadvantageous position of women. Black women, because of their circumstances, had more disadvantages to fight. Lindsay's words (1980, p.2), referring to minority ethnic women in the United States, could also apply to those in Britain: 'For minority females, programs must attempt to combat the dilemmas of sexism and racism that are inextricably linked with their depressed economic status, which often have a brutalising effect on a woman's self-concept.'

Black women felt out of place, or felt they were not wanted. In the words of Dill (1983, p.43): 'Experiences of racial oppression made Black women strongly aware of their group identity and consequently more suspicious of women, who, initially at least, defined much of their feminism in personal and individualistic terms.'

Especially in the situation of being a part of a minority group, women formed groups that satisfied their specific needs. Many such groups stood for emotional and social support, often in a strange and hostile environment. Other groups were more militant, and had specific societal agendas. The Southall Sisters have demonstrated the need for, and the benefits of grouping to fight for causes they could understand.

Agenda for Women's Studies for the next millennium

The overall aim of Women's Studies for the year 2000 onwards has to be to make women a more powerful, culturally enriched group. Thus the specific aims would be to help students to:

1. Understand what determines a woman's place in society: ie their own perceptions and expectations, upbringing, the nature of domination etc.
2. Appreciate the range of situations in which women have responded to inequality in a variety of ways, eg the case of the suffragettes, the Chipko women etc.
3. Appreciate different contexts in which issues of gender, race and class intertwine.
4. Understand the effect of racism on groups and individuals and particularly on women.
5. Enable both White and Black women to put affinity to other women above the racial contexts.
6. Be sensitive to the needs of women in different contexts.

7. Be empowered to challenge their own perceptions and conditions of living.

Relevance of content and method

The achieving of these aims means an examining of the methods and flexibility in choice of content. A traditional academic type of teaching does not maximise the potential for personnel development, which is crucial in this agenda. Women's Studies have to move from a fairly safe and secure, almost self-congratulatory framework to an all embracing one. The context of cultural diversity means that both the audience and the aims have become broader.

Implicit in a satisfactory implementation of these aims is the relevance of different women's movements and their historical context. At a personal level painful, and at the pedagogical level often shirked, is the prejudice and racism in oneself, and a realisation of the need to overcome it. Yet, if Women's Studies is to have sincerity in its appeal to all women, this needs to be tackled.

Feeling of loyalty to the women's cause is generally created by empathy, as a result of shared experience. In the words of Dill (1983, p.43): 'Sisterhood is generally understood as a nurturing, supportive feeling of attachment, and loyalty to other women has limitations in encompassing the racial and class differences among women.'

Frankenberg (1993, p.79) elaborates on this:

> There is another link between the re-conceptualisation of experience and the making of feminism, given that white feminists have often relied on notions of 'women's experience' in order to develop theory and strategy for feminism ... the experience referred to by white feminists have always been white women's experience, over generalised. Rarely and only recently have white feminists begun to examine the intersection of their gender and class positions with race privilege. Much white feminist theory generated 'from experience' has thus been flawed on two counts, very often assessing neither differences between white women of colour nor adequately describing the race-privileged positions of white women ourselves.
>
> The same points may in fact be made in relation to other groups marginalised within feminism, such as women with disabilities.

A painful agenda

The most potentially personally threatening realisation of such an approach in teaching would be, according to Lindsay (1980, p.4) the belief of Ashraf Pahlavi ('And Thus Passeth International Women's Year', *New York Times*, January 5,

1976, p.29) that: 'Understanding that one woman's stereotype of her oppressed position is another's sense of security, identity, and continuity is an insight that must be kept in mind.'

There is an additional burden on White women, as suggested by Frankenberg, (1993: p.79):

> ... the call to accountability raised by women of colour must be met in part by white women learning from one another, teaching each other, and thinking together, for example, about race privilege and its effects on feminism, rather than expecting women of colour to do all of this for us.

Unlearning racism means looking at the roots of racism. Openness is crucial, in really understanding the nature of racism and one's involvement in it. In the works of Frankenberg again:

> It is also critical, as white women examine and re-examine our complicity with racism, that we go beyond our immediate daily environments to learn more about the history of racist ideas. We need to do this in order to understand the contexts for the production of our 'racist lenses' including, for example, the ways white women 'fear' people of colour, or the way we view whiteness as 'neutral'. Reaching cognitive understandings of the history of white racist consciousness may be a valuable step towards loosening its grip on our daily lives and practice.

Frankenberg suggests there are at least three areas in which work needs to be done; a re-examining of personal history, transformation within Feminism, and active participation to bring about political change, acknowledging the deep-rootedness of racism. Her report on the reasons for, as well as success of, using personal histories is very pertinent:

> Re-examining personal history is necessary in part because it is possible that white feminists continue relating to people of colour, as well as doing feminist work, on the basis of patterns and assumptions learned early on. For example there could be a connection between white women's 'not noticing' people of colour in their childhood environments, and white feminists' capacity to continue 'forgetting' to include women of colour in the planing of conferences and events. This forgetting, may, in other words, be a socially structured one.

The thrust of much anti-racist work has been aimed at racism in White people. Frankenberg gives one reason for that (1993, p.79): '... the painful truth is that White Feminists continue to "forget", to "not think", and this means that the bulk of anti-racist work is being done by people of colour.'

On consequence of this could be to direct personal analysis at White women only. However, the differences in experience of Black and White women make it paramount that the same process is undertaken by Black women. Understanding why people are at a particular point of thought and behaviour helps one to see how one is perceived by others and this has to be a strong basis for coming together. White women have to come to terms with these attitudes, to understand how they could be a part of racism and why they could be creating a barrier for Black women. Black women need to give space for White women to be open about their views.

Empowerment

'Empowerment' has to be examined. This is a much widely used term of relevance when it consists of both the perceived oppressors and the oppressed. Empowerment is a widely used term, described by Bystydzienski (1992:3), as quoted by Yuval-Davis (1994, p.177) is: '... a process by which oppressed persons gain some control over their lives by taking part with others in the development of activities ...'

The assumption made in this chapter is that all women, not just Black women, are oppressed although for different reasons and with different consequences. Every woman is controlled and thus constrained by her socialisation. Empowerment has thus got to be a process whereby women are enabled to look freely, critically, and with confidence, at themselves, and the potential of their interaction with other women.

Solidarity, when people come from such different standpoints such as racism, feminism, class, cannot be easy. Yuval-Davis (1994, p.144) suggests that dialogue gives recognition to the: '... specific positionings of those who participate in them as well as to the "unfinished knowledge" that each such situated positioning can offer.'

The very delicate task of tutors in handling such processes cannot be emphasised too strongly.

Conclusion

The year 2000 should be a very important threshold for women. It provides us with a real opportunity to question what we have been doing and whether it is still appropriate. Both the fields of gender relations and cultural diversity have demonstrated that it is very easy for concepts and 'missions' to become traps and sources of further divisions. However, it is very important to remember Lorde's belief (1984) that we can be counter-creative if we keep on focusing on differences rather than:

... sharpen self-definition by exposing the self in work and struggle together with those whom we define as different from ourselves, although sharing the same goals. For black and white, old and young, lesbian and heterosexual women alike, this can mean new paths to survival.

Those women that are sincere about both Black and White women working together to help all women move forward will find their own experiences, ideas and practices enriched. The last part of Lorde's poem (1986), *Stations*, is the most appropriate point on which to finish:

> Some women wait for something
> to change and nothing
> does change
> so they change
> themselves

11 Teaching Women's Studies in women's prisons

Shauna Morton

This chapter offers an account of the procedures and strategies employed in order to facilitate a Women's Studies course within a prison education department. It illustrates the link between origins of misrepresentation and public understanding of Feminism generally, and Women's Studies in particular. It also offers suggestions, based on research within prison, as to how to combat the negative perceptions of Women's Studies, and asks questions about the importance of naming and reclamation.

Theories of gender have demonstrated the primacy of dominant ideologies of femininity, when explaining and examining the condition of women within society (Smith, 1990; Spender, 1989; Walby, 1992). The apparatus necessary to understand the condition of women in society is present in the concepts of patriarchy (Walby, 1992), racism (hooks, 1994) and capitalism (Barrett, 1984). Most Feminisms now attempt to merge these concepts in order to understand the complex and varied positioning of women in late capitalist western society. Gender theories which do not acknowledge the multi-faceted nature of oppressions both between, and within, women may serve to perpetuate and reinforce many of the social exclusions which operate through all or any of these concepts (Walby, 1992).

It has been argued that prisons are a microcosm of wider society (Foucault, 1977; Cohen, 1975). If we accept this analogy, then we must necessarily pursue a dynamic interpretation of the prison education experience; an experience which is fundamentally mediated by and through the social categories of gender, race and class.

In this chapter I will do as follows:

1   Present the context of women in prison.
2   Elucidate the current educational provision offered to the female prisoners in this particular prison.

3   State the pedagogical practices advocated and exemplified within the chapter.
4   Present a detailed account of the first day of a Women's Studies course, in which I illustrate the 'gap' between the reality of a Women's Studies discourse and the perceptions and assumptions held by women in prison. Demonstrate the strategies utilised in order to introduce a Feminist perspective and Women's Studies dialogue into the prison curriculum.
5   In conclusion, present strategies for Feminist pedagogical practice, which locate the classroom as a site of critical engagement and analytical freedom.

Women in Prison

In December 1995 there was an average of just over 2,150 women incarcerated in prisons in England and Wales (NACRO, 1995 Statistics bulletin). The numbers of women being sent to prison are increasing yearly, yet they remain marginalised and neglected in contemporary social theorising. The female prisoner tends to gain general recognition only through the salacious imagery of the media, which utilises a dichotomised image of imprisoned women, 'woman as victim and woman as evil' (Lloyd 1994). Dominant ideologies of femininity inform our pre-conceptions of women and offending behaviour, consequently as a society we assume women do not commit the same offences as men (Tchaikovsky 1984). The National Association for the Care and Resettlement of Offenders (NACRO) have released statistics relating to the crimes of women currently serving a custodial sentence. The following table illustrates women imprisoned according to offence:

Offence	Percentage
Violent Offences	19.4%
Theft and Handling	18.2%
Drug related Offences	23.9%
Fraud and Forgery	6.7%
Robbery	6.8%
Burglary	3.7%
Sexual Offences	0.8%
Other*	20.5%

(NACRO 1995 Prison Statistics Leaflet)

* To include all offences not covered in any of the previous categories, such as non payment of fines, disturbances, solicitation, drunk driving etc.

These statistics, from December 1995, cannot be taken as representative given the continuous turnover of women beginning and ending sentences. The figures seem to suggest that contrary to popular ideology, drug abuses, theft and violence are the major offences for which women are imprisoned. The salacious imagery of the sex industry seems not to impact significantly on the female prison population, nor does the presently favoured portrayal of 'women as victims'.

The length of time women spend in custody similarly does not accord with popular opinion. There is, it seems, a general assumption that women spend less time in prison than their male counterparts and that as women are 'naturally' less deviant than men then they receive shorter sentences. The following table demonstrates female custodial sentencing:

Up to and including 3 months	6.8%
Over 3 and up to 6 months	10.6%
Over 6 and up to 12 months	14.4%
Over 12 and up to 18 months	9.3%
Over 18 and up to 3 years	20.4%
Over 3 and up to 5 years	16.6%
Over 5 years and up to 10 years	12.9%
Over 10 years and less than life	1.3%
Life	7.7%

(NACRO December 1995)

As the figures demonstrate, well over fifty percent of women serving a custodial sentence are spending a minimum of 18 months in prison. These statistics demonstrate the need for a comprehensive educational package within women's prisons though many women are excluded when courses are over subscribed.

Currently, education is an option open to all women serving custodial sentences. The following is a list of the courses currently on offer on a full time basis at the prison in which the research is located:

Dress Making
Cookery and Catering
Hairdressing
Business Administration
Art based subjects
Access

These courses demonstrate the dominant ideological conventions which govern the lives and education of women in prison. The domestic primacy of womanhood seems integral to the pedagogical practice employed. hooks (1994) states that only through the introduction of emancipatory pedagogic practices can education (in women's prisons) devolve from its dependent domestic origins and develop practice which educates without manipulation. There is enough (necessary?) manipulation within the penal regime, perhaps it is time for an alternative.

Introducing an alternative

Pedagogic practices and curriculum utilised within the prison served to further differentiate the perceived positioning of students and staff. The polarisation of staff and students was primarily due to the complete lack of autonomy, self-reliance and power felt by the students - the demarcation was positively pursued by the staff. I was, and am, aware of the many factors which have contributed to the very marked power imbalance that exists between staff and students. The students are prisoners of the State. They are being punished; this factor alone deprives them of power (Carlen 1984, 1994, Genders and Player 1987). A penal environment is necessarily rigid, strictly regulated and governed by a seemingly endless procession of rules (Cavadino 1989). In many instances, education staff have no option but to enforce and govern these rules. I did not feel I had the same responsibility toward the prison, its rules or its current educational practices. I wanted to in some way interrupt the dominant organisation of knowledge production which seemed to reinforce and reproduce masculinist notions of female domestication and dependency.

I was offered the opportunity to intervene in the students'/prisoners' education, in order to give the students something other than sewing or cake-making. I wanted to introduce a Feminist perspective into the prison classroom by way of a Women's Studies course. Initially, this proved to be fairly problematic. Women in the prison did not want to hear about Women's Studies. They perceived it as some kind of 'soap box' for lesbians and 'men-haters'. It threatened them, which is not really surprising when consideration is given to media representations of the sexuality and sexual activities of women confirmed in prison. However, I was still determined to introduce Feminist practice, theory and politics somehow into the student curriculum. I was assuming a position more knowledgeable than that of the students. I presumed that the only reason they did not want to engage with Feminist pedagogy, and a Women's Studies discourse, was because they had no real perception of what it meant. Once they understood Feminism then they would, of course, embrace it. Adopting this superior position was in contradiction to the Feminist philosophies I espoused. How could I justify and align my masculinist hegemonic practice with the empowering philosophies of Feminism? Objectively I could not - however at the time I was willing to postpone reflections on practice, in favour of action.

Problems of naming

Taking into account the students'/prisoners' aversion to Women's Studies and Feminism, I decided to call the course an introduction to Sociology. I agonised over this decision, as I am aware of the current and continuing debates which rage over the issue of naming. Should we maintain Women's Studies, or should the less provocative, less threatening Gender Studies take precedence (Robinson

1994)? Should we abandon the name to make Women's Studies more accessible, more conformist, and more in keeping with dominant academic modes of production (Morgan 1981), thus opening up the study of women and men to all? I wanted to maintain the Women's Studies label, but to do so could result in the workshops not running due to lack of interest. I came to the conclusion that given the condition of their confinement, and the marked distancing from any form of Feminist rhetoric, the only was to run the Women's Studies course was by creating and pursuing my own 'hidden agenda' (Ilich 1969). Therefore, the course officially became 'An Introduction to Sociology'.

The process

The following sections present in detail the first day of the course. It is necessary to given an account of the pedagogical practices and the curriculum content of this day, as the continuation of the course was dependent on its success. Students had chosen this session as a voluntary option. They could leave or stay at their own discretion, therefore making it vital that they engaged with and enjoyed the first day. I feel it necessary at this point to stress the tension involved in initially employing strategies to enable emancipatory practice. The risks inherent in this type of practice, were in this instant exaggerated; if the students would not engage then I had failed completely, both them and myself. I could not try again the next day as the students would not return. However, the students did return each day, and we completed the course. It is hard to establish at this late stage who got the most out of it, the students or their tutor.

Introducing Feminist practice

At this first session there were 12 women. I was apprehensive about calling the course 'Sociology', when the material prepared was quite obviously drawn from a Women's Studies discourse. The women had a fairly eclectic mix of social class, age and ethnicity, by which I was comforted. They seemed to all intents and purposes remarkably similar to the students I taught on the Women's Studies BA at Sheffield Hallam University. I used this first session to discuss my ideas about pedagogical practice, strategies and ideologies with the students. I talked about my commitment to anti-oppressive pedagogies which allowed space for reflection and transformation. I was trying to create a space in which we all could learn and develop, to evoke personal and social change (Schniedewind and Maher 1987). I believed this process enabled both tutor and student to develop both autonomously, and as part of the group (hooks 1994, Robinson 1993, Epstein 1993). This was all very new to the women. Therefore, it took them a while to engage with the discussion, and initially there was a lot of confusion and scepticism: 'We can't work like that, what are you saying that you want to learn too, well then you shouldn't be a teacher, nobody will know what to do.' (Anna)

I had expected this type of resistance. Feminist, and other literature has documented the problems encountered when trying to introduce new emancipatory practices into the classroom (see hooks 1994, Freire 1977). I explained that we would adopt specific strategies and procedures with which we could unpack and deconstruct 'accepted' knowledges. We would develop new ways of critically looking at and addressing 'what we knew'. Furthermore, I stressed that they have knowledge that they could share, and that knowledge was as valid as any other. There was a reluctant acceptance of this and from this point on we discussed whatever came up; prison, children, education, courts and magistrates. As the students could not categorise what they were doing easily, every now and then one of them would ask 'but what are we doing, what are we supposed to be learning, when do we start.' (Colleen) As the morning progressed the question was asked less and less, the last time one of the women asked it, another student replied,'oh shut up, this is what we're doing, we're talking about things which are important to us, we hardly ever do this so leave it along.'(Betsy) There was general agreement to this and the discussions carried on through the morning. Just before the women left for their lunch break, I asked them to reflect on our discussions and to try and identify one new 'thing' they had learned that morning.

I was pleased with the morning session. There is a general tendency to assume that women in prison are stupid, slow, and not very bright (Dobash et al 1985, Zedner 1994). However, many women in prison are bright, articulate and mentally agile, and this I think was demonstrated particularly well within the morning session through their ability to adapt and feel comfortable with new practices in such a short space of time. A further factor for my pleasure over the seeming success of the morning session became apparent. As we were working within a pretty tight schedule (initially the course was to run for two weeks, and if it was successful there was the possibility of running it on a more permanent regulated basis), I did not want to continue deceiving the students about the content and underlying philosophy of the course as that could undermine the emancipatory political nature of Feminism and Women's Studies. I therefore decided to introduce the concept and ideology of Feminism in the afternoon session. Being fundamentally influenced by bell hooks' (1994) notion of education as the 'practice of freedom', I did not believe the course would survive if it was mediated through deception; they deserved the opportunity to reject or accept from an informed position.

Introducing Women's Studies

The afternoon session was vital in that it was here that the course would 'live or die'. All the women returned for the afternoon session and brought a further seven women with them. This I perceived initially as presenting problems. I had spent all morning getting the women relaxed and comfortable and willing to talk within a classroom setting. I had identified the leaders and listeners in the group, and I had an idea about how well the group would operate as 'a group'. All this was shot to pieces with the arrival of seven new members. My first instinct was to turn them away, however I quickly realised that to do this would alienate me from the rest of the group. Women in prison learn to distrust very quickly. I had no choice but to accommodate all the women. I had prepared a series of questions which the women had to discuss. Using standard seminar formats, I divided the women up into groups, gave them the discussion sheets and some A1 paper and asked them to discuss.

The discussion sheets focused their attention on issues around Feminism and Women's Studies. It asked for their perceptions of Women's Studies as an educational pursuit and the what, who, when and where of Feminism. The emphasis was placed quite firmly on their understanding, and how they perceived these issues. I assured them there were no right answers only opinions. The majority of the women did not initially want to engage with the issues, however after a lot of discussion which concentrated on the validity of their opinions and their right to express them, they agreed to co-operate with the proviso that if they became bored we would adopt a different strategy and focus point.

The virtually unanimous condemnation of Feminism and Women's Studies that arose from their group discussions, was expected. An analysis of their critique highlighted three distinct underlying themes. The first of these is encapsulated perfectly in these statements: 'Feminists are a bunch of men-hating dykes who really just want to be men.' (Group One, Anna, Betsy, Colleen and Dorothy). This statement, whilst one of the most extreme, demonstrated the low esteem in which anything located specifically within the female realm was held by the women. Women's Studies was perceived as outside standard educational practices, therefore a waste of time. 'Why do Women's Studies, when we know what its like to be a women and don't need any homosexual group to tell us.' (Group Two, Erica, Fiona, Greta, Hannah and Ina). The continuous alignment of Feminism and Women's Studies with a specific sexuality demanded further examination. Why did the women couple these two positions? As most of the women seemed to concur with this notion, it became vital to investigate where their information came from.

A further theme which developed during the feedback sessions which deserved more consideration was put by a small group of women, who seemed to have been most influenced by one group member who was extremely well educated, and had a stream of academic qualifications.

> The problem with Feminism and Women's Studies is that they are only for white middle class women, who really have nothing better to do with their

time, so they create this little clique which effectively excludes anyone who isn't like them
(Group Five, Jane, Katherine and Linda).

This I felt was a reasoned critique, and has had many supporters within Feminism (hooks 1989, Lorde 1987). However, I felt it was a misinformed analysis of the diversity of contemporary Feminism and Women's Studies. Moreover, this group had taken the time to consider the issues around Feminism. As this was about women's experiences, I felt it would be inappropriate to utilise the knowledge I had gained through reading the literature on exclusionary practices and elitism within Feminism and Women's Studies to contradict their statement. Furthermore, additional discussion around this point did produce the next emergent theme which was differentiation, women and 'race'.

Consequently, by the end of the feedback sessions I had identified three major themes; sexuality, differentiation and representation (gaze). These three themes emerged repeatedly throughout all the sessions, and as a group we explored, unpacked and minutely analysed them. However, presenting a detailed account of these themes is not within the remit of this chapter, although it is an area I am exploring within my PhD thesis.

Conclusions and strategies for practice

In summing up, I want to focus on the use of experiential knowledge to validate theory and perspective. The success of the first day of this course was vital to its continuation, which is why I have presented it in such detail. Emancipatory practice, where the development of student autonomy is a necessary pre-requisite, is a frightening prospect for any tutor first engaging with this standpoint. Drawing extensively from hooks' (1994) notion of 'Education as the Practice of Freedom', I endeavoured to enable and empower the students whilst still guiding them. We did this by applying theory only through their ground experiences and by using their own knowledge to elucidate and illuminate many of the abstract conceptual issues inherent in the study of women in society.

Lewis (1990) contends that in most classroom interaction there are 'pedagogical moments' which arise within specific contexts which contribute to the development of counter-hegemonic practices (Lewis 1990). I would argue that this is fundamentally so within the Feminist classroom. Without such moments of critical and analytical awareness, which lead to both social and personal transformation, the Feminist classroom remains within mainstream education, and necessarily loses the politicising impact of its Feminisms.

Influenced by hooks and Lewis, I believe it is possible to identify in the first day of this Women's Studies course the pedagogical moments which enabled the successful continuation of the course, and in so doing, serve to demonstrate the fundamental impact the experience of being involved had on the lives of both the students and their tutor.

Pedagogical moments or Feminist strategies

The strategies I employed to facilitate the creation of an environment which was conducive to the emancipatory vision of Feminist pedagogy were as follows:

> The creation of an open space - permission must be initially given to the students to take over the space. This was particularly difficult in the prison as the regime requires total and absolute control. Therefore, it was necessary to negotiate with them on a continuous basis the amount of control and the levels of power they felt comfortable with, and then offer them a little more than they requested. This was not done overtly, but by the gradual dispersion of responsibility between us.
>
> Hostility and resistance to new practices are common place. It was essential that objections are taken seriously, and that they inform related considered discussions. By doing this the women realised that their words were important, their feelings accepted and their view of the world valid. Without this non-judgemental standpoint the course would have undoubtedly failed.

An afterthought: Women in prison occupy a particular position in society; an unenviable position which relegates them to perhaps the lowest rung of social hierarchies. Their lives are strictly regulated, overseen and controlled. Our diversion into a Women's Studies discourse enabled the women to examine why they occupied this social position, how formal and informal controls mediated their experiences and to what extent they had accepted a contradictory view of themselves. They became angry, sad, exited, loud. The further into the course we went, the more risks they took, with each other, with me, with the prison authorities (an unfortunate side effect) but most of all with themselves. We were told that unfortunately there was not the funding available to run the course on a permanent basis, which saddened me, but angered the women - who should have the last word:

> This has been brilliant, I've learned more here that I have in all the education I've been to in the two years I've been inside. It's typical - they find one thing that you really want to do and they take it away from you.

12 Women's Studies in Continuing Education: the Sussex experience

Gerry Holloway

Women's Studies in this country developed from the Women's Movement of the 1960s and 1970s and began in the extra-mural departments of Universities and in the Worker's Education Association (WEA). The first courses tended to have generalised titles such as 'Women in Society'; 'Women and Work'; 'Women and the Family' etc. My first teaching experience was on a Women's Studies course organised by the Women's Section of the Brighton WEA in the mid 1980s. Texts used were written by well-known feminists of the time such as Kate Millet, Adrienne Rich, Sheila Rowbotham, Juliet Mitchell, Sally Alexander and Shulamith Firestone. Since those days there has been a debate over whether Women's Studies is an extension of the Women's Movement or if, as Susan Sheridan has argued (1990, p.36), 'It is now structurally (and some would maintain, ideologically) distinct from that movement.'

This may be true of Women's Studies in Higher Education, but I believe that Women's Studies in Continuing Education (CE) has maintained stronger links with the Women's Movement and in some ways operates as a bridge between the academic world of Women's Studies in Higher Education and the social and political movement.

In this chapter, I want to explore this contention by focusing on the institution I know best, the University of Sussex. I do not want to draw any universal conclusions about the relationship between the Women's Movement and Women's Studies from this narrow examination but just offer some points for discussion. Such a discussion would, I think, be useful as Women's Studies in CE is not usually the focus of mainstream feminist collections on the state of Women's Studies - for example the yearly collections published by the Women's Studies Network.

I shall begin by describing briefly the role of CE in the world of tertiary education, in particular the area formerly known as Liberal Adult Education as this is the area in which Women's Studies is largely situated. I shall then discuss some of the developments that have occurred over the last few years which have led to the accreditation of most CE courses and the implications this has had for adult learners. This will be followed by an examination of the development of Women's Studies at the Centre for Continuing Education (CCE) at the University of Sussex. This will lead into a discussion of the relationship between Women's Studies in CE at Sussex and the courses available in the rest of the University. I then hope to open up the discussion to widen the area of focus to ascertain whether there is any currency in my contention that Women's Studies in CE is possibly closer to the social and political Women's Movement than Women's Studies in Higher Education.

Continuing Education

Continuing Education is aimed at part-time students over the age of 21. Courses are taught on campus or in other venues such as Adult Education Centres, Community Centres and Further Education Colleges throughout the region during the day, evenings or weekends. The levels of courses are various. This was less important when most were seen as having intrinsic value. Students traditionally come from a wide range of backgrounds because of the open access policy. The heterogeneity of CE classes means that when they work well, classes are dynamic and intensely stimulating; when they are less successful they can be rather disjointed and disappointing to the participants.

I do not propose to go through the whole history of CE here but I want to indicate its relationship to the rise of the Women's and Labour Movement. CE has its roots in the campaign for University Extension which began in the mid-nineteenth century. Interestingly, this campaign was linked to the Feminist campaign to open up secondary and higher education for women.

In 1899, Ruskin College was founded and in 1903, the WEA. The purpose of Ruskin College was to provide relevant education and training for working-class leaders and the curriculum mainly comprised History, Economics and Political Science. The WEA proved popular because of its use of tutorial classes rather than formal lectures. This type of provision was called Liberal Adult Education. The philosophy of Liberal Adult Education was based on what Harold Wiltshire (WEA founder) defined as 'The Great Tradition'. This was characterised by:

- A commitment to humane/liberal studies;
- An especial concern for social studies as a way of understanding the great issues of modern life;
- A non-vocational attitude;
- A non-selective provision which has democratic notions of the educability of adults;
- An adoption of the Socratic method in its use of small tutorial groups and guided discussion.

Over the years there have been many challenges and changes to Liberal Adult Education but the only one I want to mention is the most recent accreditation. This has had a profound impact on the whole character of CE and, implicit in that, Women's Studies within CE. In 1993, in line with the Government's intention to transform Higher Education, the Higher Education Funding Council of England (HEFCE) changed its funding policy for CE and stated that the Council 'wishes to encourage as much non-vocational continuing education as possible to become (if not already) award-bearing or to carry credits towards an award.' (HEFCE, January 1994, p.6)

Most courses run by CE departments in England were non-accredited. Moreover, there was a common assumption that students were against accreditation. In 1993 Patricia Ambrose and I were awarded a Research Fellowship to examine the effect on funding changes on the provision of Liberal Adult Education (LAE). Contrary to the belief that LAE classes comprised of a wider range of students, we found that by 1993, they were being attended by women over 50. These women had formal qualifications and were largely resistant to the idea of accreditation. Many students felt that they did not want or need credit and others were nervous about having to do exams. However, changes in funding policy meant that most of our courses would have to be changed into accredited courses which would have to be at least Higher Education level one to attract funding.

Women's Studies in the Centre for Continuing Education at the University of Sussex

Although some people felt depressed about the changes, they did offer a new opportunity for some subject areas and, in particular, the field of Women's Studies. At this time (1993), the Centre for Continuing Education offered very few Women's Studies courses. In 1992, some 'New Horizons for Women' courses had successfully run and my colleague, Mary Stuart, developed a part-time Access to Higher Education course. This was specifically focused on Women's Studies as a pathway to Higher Education for New Horizons students and others from the Liberal Adult programme and elsewhere. The curriculum consisted of Literature, Sociology, Women's History and Study Skills. I taught the History component and the programme ran very successfully for three years until we were forced to discontinue the programme when yet another change in funding policy situated Access provision in the FE sector. Fortunately, a new Women's Studies Access course has been developed by a local Sixth Form College.

During the first year of the Access course, I took over from a colleague who was developing a Certificate in Women's Studies as part of the Centre's response to the HEFCE circular through a programme of award-bearing courses to complement our shortly-to-be accredited Liberal Studies programme. As well as needing to meet the requirements of the funding council, we wanted to develop a range of Women's Studies courses which would offer women pathways to full-time Higher Education or post-graduate work if they so desired; or offer them a place where they could explore women's issues in a supportive environment.

The Certificate in Women's Studies is a part-time evening course taught, at present, on the campus of the University of Sussex. Tutors and students meet for 2 hours a week for ten weeks over three terms. Students are given help with study skills by the course tutor in the first instance and if they have more serious problems they are referred to our education Equality Unit where they can receive one-to-one help. One feature of the programme is that there are no unseen exams. Courses are assessed by essay, oral presentation, project work and short pieces of criticism.

Students come from a wide range of backgrounds and ages. Some already have a degree and want to update their knowledge, especially if they covered very little feminist theory in their degree. These women sometimes go on to take the MA in Women's Studies. Others have a professional interest or engage in activities and work which relate to women. Others are solely interested in current developments in feminist theory. Quite a few wish to use the course as a step towards further academic qualifications. The University is a member of the Southern Universities Credit Accumulation and Transfer Scheme, a group of universities including Sussex, Kent, Southampton, Surrey and the Open University, which recognise credit from each other's courses. Therefore students can, and do, use their credits to do a degree either full-time or part-time. The courses are also open as free-standing courses for students on degree courses, for example the part-time degree in Cultural Studies or as a special subject for overseas visiting students. Moreover, if the students do well in all the courses of the Diploma they can be interviewed for a place on the MA in Women's Studies, which is organised by another department, without a first degree.

The enrolment for this year gives one a clear indication of the range of women who take the course. Out of an intake of eighteen students, we have two English teachers from Japan who want to take an award that will help them widen their students' understanding of British culture; a graduate from Brazil who wants to do the programme while her husband is doing postgraduate research here; a Portuguese undergraduate who is taking this programme and another award-bearing programme as her study year abroad, a Black American student and a Vietnamese American student who are taking one term as part of their study year abroad, four women who are doing the course because they work with women and want to learn about feminist theory, three women who left school at fifteen or sixteen and want to eventually enter Higher Education and three women who state they want to do the programme for interest only. Apart from the overseas students, students come from all over the region. Ages range from their early twenties to late fifties and in the past we have also had retired women doing the programme. Moreover, there is a sliding scale of fees so that we have a fair number of students on income support.

The profile of students is very different to that of the old days of non-accredited Liberal Adult Education classes dominated by elderly, white, educated women. I must add however that Women's Studies classes have always been the most heterogeneous of all our courses.

We still cater for this earlier group of students, offering day school and accredited weekly courses sometimes in connection with the WEA or University of the Third Age. Further, I have just developed an introductory weekly accredited course called 'The Changing Experience of Women' which is aimed at women wanting to take award-bearing programmes but lacking the confidence, or women who are just interested to find out more about the subject. This course is based in Literature, Creative Writing, Sociology, History, Life History and Study Skills and we shall be using local resources to explore women's lives.

Students who have finished or are finishing the programme want more, so we have also developed a range of Day schools for past, present and future students. We also encourage students to use their skills either in their workplace or by becoming involved in local and national women's issues. I used to encourage students to subscribe to *Everywoman* and they participated in various campaigns from reading that late-lamented publication. Some also become members of the regional or national Women's History Network.

Some advantages and disadvantages of Women's Studies in CE

I teach Women's Studies both in CCE and in the main university on the MA in Women's Studies, so I have a broad perspective of the advantages and disadvantages of Women's Studies in CE.

- The main advantage of teaching Women's Studies in CCE is that it is student driven to a large extent. By that I mean that courses are run at times that suit students. Student numbers (maximum 18) are small enough for their needs to be identified and, where possible, attended to and courses are developed in response to student demand.
- Teaching adults means that students bring their varied experiences to the curse which makes seminars lively if somewhat difficult to manage at times. Students are also very committed to the course, not least because they are paying for it.
- Although courses on the award-bearing programme have to be approved by Senate, there has been little difficulty in getting this approval and weekly courses and day schools only have to pass a departmental committee. Fortunately, as the committee is sympathetic to Women's Studies, constraints are only financial so we are fairly flexible in our programming.

However, although Women's Studies is flourishing in CCE, it suffers from some problems which are common to everyone in CE:

- Although there are students who want more courses and tutors willing to offer new ones, funding constraints make it difficult to develop any more courses for the award-bearing programme at present unless we drop existing ones. Consequently, my hopes to develop a part-time degree in Women's Studies is on hold for the foreseeable future. However, I have some leeway with weekly courses and Day Schools which means we can still offer subjects not covered in the award-bearing programme.
- I would like the tutors to have more job security. Most are termly paid, part-time tutors. This is often tolerable when the tutor is a post graduate student or has other employment but, for me, part of the stress of the job is not being able to give tutors as much work as they would like. I also have lists of would-be tutors whom I cannot employ.
- I also regret that there are no grants or bursaries available for part-time students at the moment. However, I am investigating the possibility of applying for EU funding for courses aimed at specific groups of women, such as unemployed women, ethnic minorities, women in rural areas etc.
- Further, the move to accreditation has meant a move from the margins of the University closer to the mainstream. This had its advantages because our award-bearing programme students have access to all the privileges of full-time students, eg access to the library, student union etc. However, it has also meant that we have had to comply with regulations which are aimed at full-time students and these can make life difficult, especially if students study off-campus and access to the campus is difficult because of travel problems. This means that we are in constant negotiation with administration over issues such as extended deadlines, return of library books, intermissions etc. Consequently, our flexibility is constrained.
- There is also a danger that as part-time and full-time students become more amalgamated into mainstream and CE courses, our individuality could become subsumed by the wider university. This could mean that the special needs of adult part-time students could be overlooked as they will be a minority rather than the main group. This would be a shame because at the moment it is possible to have a close relationship with students and work together on issues beyond the programme curriculum. For example, another programme is publishing a book on their research with the help of their convenor.

We also share problems that Women's Studies in Higher Education suffer from. Like the postgraduate Women's Studies at Sussex we do not have a 'home' of our own for research. My contributions to the Research Assessment Exercise were counted under Education this time. However, if there is another round, my current research and publications will be placed under History. Other members of faculty in the main part of the university found work placed largely under Sociology. This has resource implications for Women's Studies and from what I have read or heard about other institutions this problem is widespread.

Conclusion

Women's Studies in CE is intimate and friendships and networks are created which really reflect the personal as political. As Convenor, I feel it is important to encourage students to develop in ways which suit them. For some, it might be entrance into undergraduate or graduate courses, for others it might be encouraging them to participate in a political or social issue they are interested in. The students, initially with our encouragement, are supportive of each other and arrange out-of-course social and political activities.

Evaluation forms from students refer to gaining confidence and a heightened awareness of women's issues through their studies. Several have become involved in women's campaigns. Some students are school teachers and use the course to inform their teaching. Others are considering a change of career to something that focuses on women's issues.

Students come to the programme with a wide range of experience and often are looking for ways to understand and articulate that experience. This gives them a sense of mutuality which is not always the case in Higher Education where student numbers are often high and there is little sense of continuity because groups disperse every term. In Higher Education tutors are usually teaching Women's Studies alongside other courses and often cannot give as much time to students needs as I can as Convenor of Women's Studies in CE. This continuity helps students develop the confidence they need to go on to activity outside of the institution.

So I contend that Women's Studies in CE in my institution at least is linked to the political aims of the Women's Movement. Mature students are more likely to be settled in the community than younger more mobile women and some turn to their community to put their theoretical knowledge and research skills to use. Most of the students do not expect to have a professional academic career and are often more focused on issues rather than the finer points of Feminist theory. Fortunately, programmes, at the moment, are fairly flexible and we can accommodate students by focusing on current issues. I would now like to open up a discussion on whether academic Women's Studies has become divorced from the political movements and whether the relationship, if it exists is a useful one.

13 Window on The Netherlands

Greet Goverde

This chapter begins with a comparative study of the participation in education of British and Dutch adult women. The results left me with more questions than I started with. So to broaden understanding, I will tell you about the Dutch educational system, including Women's Studies and current Feminist debate in the Dutch media.

I have also made use of experience gained in exchange visits between Nijmegen (The Netherlands) and Swindon (Wiltshire). During the first exchange we focussed on the social structure in the two countries; during the second exchange the subject was a conveniently wide field: emancipation: ethnicity, class and gender. We visited comparable areas of town, cultural, Feminist and ethnic organisations, had talks and workshops and discussions of course.

Comparison of participation in education of British and Dutch adult women

Before I began this study my impression was that at British universities a larger proportion of the student population were adult women (or adults, period) than in Dutch universities. This was based on what I heard and saw during exchange visits in 1993 and 1994 between Nijmegen Community College and Swindon College. Why did the women I saw in Swindon appear to be more actively preparing for university and other forms of Higher Education than our own students? If more British students went on to university, why was that? First of course I had to check the 'if'.

Young people

This is the generally known picture of British education compared to the same age category in The Netherlands:

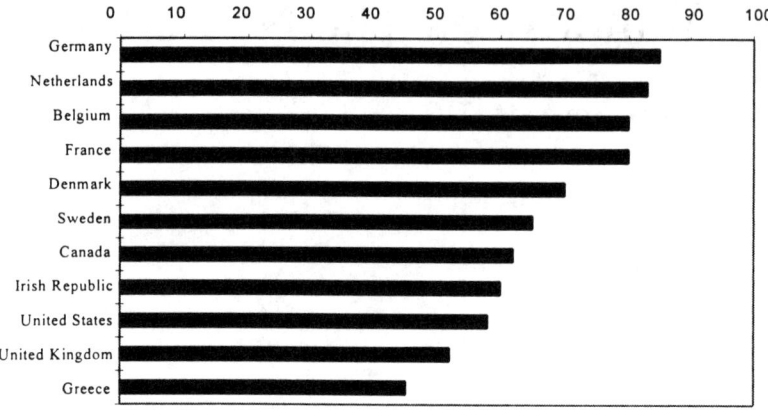

Figure 1 Percentage of 18 year olds in education and training: International comparison 1992
Source: OECD

So my expectations that there would be fewer young people in universities and other forms of Higher Education in the UK, were confirmed.

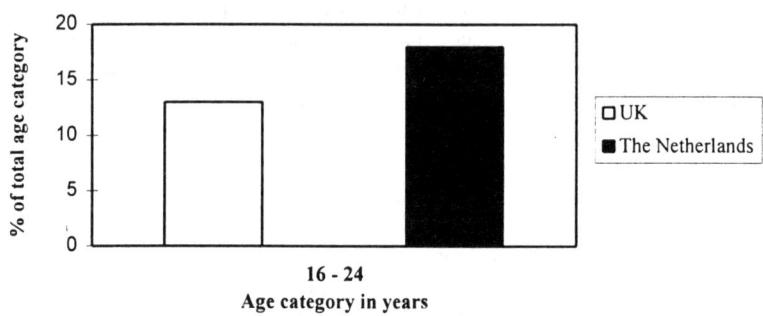

Figure 2 Students at Universities and other Institutes for Higher Education 1993/94 (OU excluded)
Sources : CBS, DFEE

However, the next diagram shows a different picture:

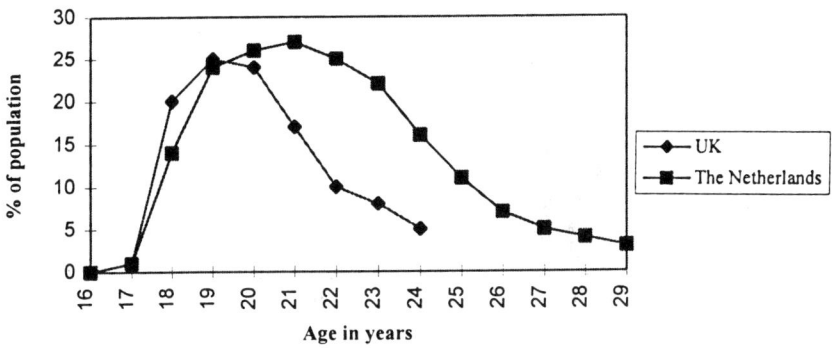

Figure 3 Age and Higher Education
1993/94 Sources: CBS & HMSO

The *number* of British young people who follow university and other Higher Education does not differ greatly from the number of Dutch students. The difference lies in the time they spend at the different institutions, and in the fact that they start at different ages (eg in The Netherlands: after military service, or after making the detour lower vocational - secondary vocational - higher vocational). In a few years' time this picture will probably look different: the Dutch government is shortening the period of study.

Mature students

Unfortunately I have only managed to match the numbers for those over the age of 25; see diagram below. The categories for smaller age-groups, gender, sorts of education etc. kept diverging again. To these figures should be added the eleven per cent of British students in centres for Further Education. The results as regards the comparable number of 'adult' students surprised me, as the grant-system is rather more forbidding in The Netherlands: over 27 you do not receive a grant, whereas in Britain mature students receive extra. Apparently the Dutch find the money elsewhere. Probably the more favourable economic situation makes things easier.

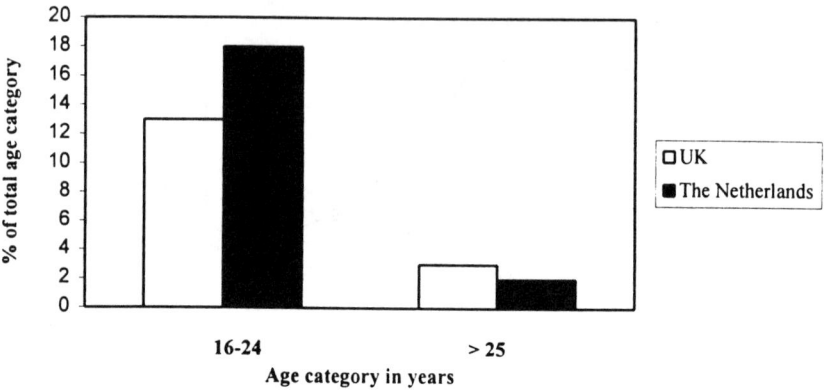

Figure 4 Students at Universities and other Institutes for Higher Education

Women and men

As regards the *gender difference* it was not possible to match the data exactly. The data indicate that the situation in the two countries is comparable:

- Men tend to take full-time courses, women part-time courses
- Men tend to study science subjects, women the humanities subjects
- Overall, the numbers of male-female students do not differ greatly.

I had a look at the numbers of adult students at Nijmegen University. I observed:

- A sudden drop at age 27, as could be expected (no more grants).
- 30 - 40 : three men to every two women
- 40 - 50 : almost the same.
- 50 - 60 : more than twice as many women.
- 60 and older: more men, with a sudden rise at age 65 (retirement age).

As regards the age-group 50 - 60, they are probably women whose children have left home and who now take their second chance. This is my own age group. I was the youngest in the family and the first girl to get secondary and Higher Education. 'It's a pity it's her whose got the good brain, and not her brother' I heard an uncle say. It made me feel as if I had something which was not rightfully mine, as if I had stolen something. My two elder sisters learnt good housekeeping and accounting. They were needed as extra pairs of hands in our inn (the family business), and that was my luck: by the time I was of that age I was not needed. Most of my classmates left school at fourteen or sixteen to work in a shop or in the family business or farm, or in an office. When they got in a shop or in the family business or farm, or in an office. When they got married they stayed at home, as their mothers did. I do not remember any of my classmates' mothers going out to work other than one or two who were cleaners a few mornings a week. Traditionally women in The Netherlands stayed at home much more than in other countries, cleaning and scrubbing. Dutch housewives were notorious for that. This has changed surprisingly quickly, within one generation: the younger generation of women get an education, then a job if they can, and have children at the highest age in Europe.

Women at Nijmegen Community College

How do the adult women at the community college where I teach English feel about the fact that there are no grants for them after 27? With a colleague I did a quick survey among this year's students of 19 women aged 22 or less who took Havo and VWO (= A-level) English exams at Nijmegen Community College in 1996.

Reasons for studying (some ticked more than one category)

10	Personal interest ('keeping up with the children', 'personal development', 'hobby' etc.)
11	Preparation for Higher Education.

Financial prospects

9	Did not expect financial problems because of job ('I have saved') / grant + job / husband who pays, etc.
2	Said they were entitled to grants the first few years (until 27) but would have to tackle financial problems after that.
4	Said they would have liked to go on to Higher Education but could not do so for financial reasons. (low income, support children.

One of the students remarked:

> I'm not entitled to grants. This year I got one VWO-certificate. In this way it will take me years to get a diploma. If finance didn't play a role I would immediately stop working and get my certificates and go to university after all.

Conclusion to Comparative Study

I do not know whether it is easier or more difficult for British women over 22 to enter university or HE. I should have thought it was easier, because of this extra allowance for people over 26, but it did not show up in the responses. The Dutch system is not fair to mature women (and men) who have not taken or have not been able to take the opportunity to study at an earlier age.

Surprisingly, this unfairness is not a matter for debate in The Netherlands. Perhaps because most people find a way to continue their studies: wages and allowances in The Netherlands are higher. And there is always the Open University. So it is only a small group of people who have this problem.

The Dutch education system

Giving an impression of the state of affairs in education with reference to Women's Studies in The Netherlands was the reason I have been asked to contribute to *Into the Melting Pot*. And I welcomed the opportunity. As students of English we were told by one of the lecturers that we were supposed to become a sort of ambassadors for England, we would not only teach your language but also about your country, your culture. Well, as an ambassador for your country I have become a bit frustrated in the course of the years because I did not like everything I saw in Britain, and also because it is such a one-way traffic. Many people in my country and in other countries speak English and read books in English and watch the two BBC channels so they can form their own picture of Great Britain. But who sees us? You hear about us from the tabloids, and even on Question Time I have heard the most awful prejudices about my country. But because of the language you cannot watch our television and read our papers, and see for yourself. The British used to be insular because of their island position and now it is because of their language being the *lingua franca*.

Secondary Education

Age 12 - 15: basic education.	2 or 3 foreign languages, and mathematics obligatory.
'Havo' until 17 (preparation for higher vocational)	6 subjects
'VWO' until 18 (preparation for university)	7 subjects

In both Havo and VWO:

- Dutch and one foreign language obligatory. Strong pressure on taking at least one mathematics subject as examination subjects.

- Creative subjects obligatory until 15, later optional, as examination subjects. Physical Education obligatory until the penultimate year.

Generally speaking in the Netherlands there are:

- Fewer social activities.
- More exam-subjects, a 'broader' education.
- The subjects in British A-level courses are studied 'in depth': Maybe that is why in Great Britain university normally lasts only three years.
- Subjects within the 'normal' range of school-subjects (no law, politics, etc).
- Less stress on coursework and essays.
- No private education. All schools are state-funded except boarding schools for children whose parents live abroad.
- A large variety in schools as regards denomination or pedagogical principles, especially in primary schools, but also in secondary schools. Schools founded on certain pedagogical principles are for example Montessori, Jena-plan, Freinet, Dalton etc. These are also state-funded.

Adults (at Colleges for Further Education):

- Those over 21 need only three Havo or VWO subjects for entrance to Higher Education, depending on the faculty's demands.
- Adults take the same courses and exams as young people; no specially designed 'Access' courses.

Partly this is pure necessity: a high level of English is necessary because English textbooks have to be read in many faculties. The idea in British Access courses is that the work experience you have has also given you a valuable form of education. You are expected to build on that in the many essays you have to write. You have to prove that you can think and write sensibly about certain subjects. English students we talked to thought that what we do (adults studying the same things as young people) was silly, a waste of time. 'Why cram for several subjects when you're only going to study one at university? It's more important to learn how to formulate your own worthwhile ideas.' Some English teachers however thought the level of some of their Access students was not really high enough to take a university course.

Tertiary education

Secondary education exams: HE entrance

- No entrance exams, interviews etc. for admission to university + HE.

- All students with a Havo-diploma are admitted to higher vocational courses.
- All students with a VWO diploma are admitted to university.
- For certain subjects you have to have certain subjects in your 'packet'.
- Some studies (eg medicine, dentistry, veterinary surgery) allow only a limited number of students.
- System of 'weighted lots': more chance if your marks are higher.
- A student's choice is usually based on his or her preference for a certain town or city, for all universities offer more or less the same quality. Some specialise in certain subjects.

University and higher vocational courses:

- In The Netherlands for every student in University two go to higher vocational colleges, where you study journalism, teacher training etc. The term 'university' is reserved for the more academic, research-oriented studies.
- All courses take four years. (Reduced from 6 to 4 years over the last 6 or 7 years)
- All students get the same grants from the national government, whichever university or other HE course they take.

Grants

The Dutch system is rather simple compared to the British system with its mandatory and discretionary awards, access funds, assisted studentship, extra allowance for older students, bursaries for nurse education, awards for paramedical courses, postgraduate awards, sponsorships, etc. In The Netherlands everybody age 18-27 pays exactly the same fees and gets the same grants, whether in university or in other Higher Education:

- College fees: £930 a year plus books.
- Every student gets a free transport pass.
  (one can apply for a pass that is valid either at weekends or on weekdays)
- Grants only for people between 18 and 27 years of age.
- *All* the money has to be paid back if certain standards are not met. ('achievement grant')

If the requirements are met <u>part</u> of the amount (the loan) has to be paid back after the course if the ex-student earns an income that is above a certain minimum.

	'Low Income' Parents		'High Income' Parents	
	Living Elsewhere	Living at Parents' House	Living Elsewhere	Living at Parents' House
Basic grant[*]	160	47	160	47
Extra grant[*]	150	135	0	0
Loan	137	137	287[#]	272[#]
Total	**447**	**319**	**447**	**319**

[*] Must be paid back in case of low achievement
[#] Usually paid by parents

There are also grants for young people age 18-27 who are still studying but <u>not</u> (yet) in Higher Education.

- £68 per month when living at home,
- £158 when living away from home.
- They have to pay for their education: about £30 a month.

Women's Studies

Women's Studies
- Is not taught as a subject in secondary education.
- In the university in my town, Nijmegen, there is a Centre for Women's Studies where you can find the office of the professor, the secretaries and the documentation centre. The rest of the staff have their offices within the different faculties. They are in the first place members of the Arts faculty, the philosophy faculty etc, and can teach Women's Studies as subsidiary subjects in their own faculties.
- Compared to the furore of the seventies the Feminist movement is almost dead and gone in The Netherlands. What happens at the universities is rather academic. On the other hand Feminist issues have seeped into many aspects of everyday life, eg a few years ago the exam subject for <u>all</u> history students (including boys, including my 'poor' son) was 'the history of Feminism'.

Current Feminist debate

As stated above, the degree of participation in *paid jobs* was traditionally very low in The Netherlands, and this has its effects even now:

- Only 5% of the mothers are full time working mothers (European lowest)
- 56% are full time housewives (European highest)

There are very few women in high positions. Perhaps because the people who should appoint them are usually men who mistrust them because they are not 'normal' women like their own wives, who are at home or do volunteer work or have a small part-time job.

Young women are now better educated than boys, but end up in flexible, part-time jobs. This is because *they so wish*: they do not want a career, they do not want to join the rat-race.

So women are not making (or do not want to make?) much headway as regards 'good' jobs.

This Spring there was a debate in the papers between:

1. The new emancipated.
   (Are we emancipated? Yes!; are we Feminists? No!)
   The arguments used were that there was still inequality in work but this will be solved. Feminists therefore should not nag about it. After all women have a choice. They can opt for a career. Many do not. Furthermore, it will solve itself in time. Equality in education has been achieved in 20 years - equality in work will follow in a few decades when the present generation of male personnel officers is gone.

2. The new Feminists: (Are we Feminists? Yes!; Are we emancipated? No!)
   They defend themselves against the arguments mentioned above on the grounds that there is no more choice. 42% of heterosexual couples want to share work and care equally, but only 2% manage to do so. Furthermore, in 1977 women had 79% of men's wages, now this has fallen to 75%. Instead of nagging Feminists there are lots of nagging questions.

3. There are others who reason that the debate about these issues has not stopped but goes on at a different, more public level; on the grounds that these issues have been promoted from the Feminist agenda to the general political debate, and are part of the bargaining that goes on in politics and industrial relations.

They have been integrated into public life in a rather sensible way. One example is the history of Feminism incorporated into the national exams of all history students, including boys. (One should remember here that more young people take history than in Britain because all young people have to take seven subjects.)

Another example is the Bill which has been introduced by the Green Left party and which has already been passed in the Second Chamber, but not yet in the

First Chamber (equivalent of the House of Lords, but without Lords). This is the Bill giving everybody who has been in a full time job for a year the right to demand shorter working hours (and relinquish pay). This is especially meant to accommodate the men who say 'I'd like to spend more time at home but my boss won't let me work less.' It would help heterosexual couples to share work and care more equally.

The Bill was helped on the way by myself; it was already under discussion but I took care it was included in the local amendments to the Green Left Manifesto, and at a national congress I even climbed the rostrum to defend it (weak knees!) It got enough votes and became part of 'our' programme.

Conclusion

I realise that Feminist debate and the study of 'Women's Studies' are much more alive and lively in Britain than in the Netherlands. I am not sure, however, in which country women are better off, I tend to bet on the Netherlands, in spite of the fact that the circumstances are more favourable in Britain for mature women who want to study.

14 Globalising the 'gender agenda': a critical view of liberal Feminism in the post-Beijing order

Jenny Clegg

'Mainstreaming gender issues' has become the catchphrase of the 'post-Beijing Order'. This trend gained impetus from the publication in 1995 of the UNDP's Human Development Report calling for governments to revise their national accounts to include women's unpaid labour. This report was very influential in the framing of the Platform of Action (POA) adopted at the UN Fourth World Conference on Women in Beijing in September 1995.

But what exactly is the role of this 'gender agenda' in the current phase of globalisation? The following discussion aims to unravel the liberal feminist underpinnings of this strategy for 'engendering human development' and to demonstrate its consistency with the current global agendas of economic and political liberalisation.

Women from developing countries have voiced criticisms that the 'gender agenda' is an imposition of both the male-dominated IMF and UN (Magarey, 1995, p.146). For such feminist activists, women's collective action is the most effective response to the deterioration of women's conditions under the impact of global market forces.

The official UN Conference on Women and the parallel Non-Governmental Organisation (NGO) Forum in Beijing made visible to the world that the women's movement is now more international, more diverse, more powerful. However, at the same time as the women's movement has taken up international political issues, international agendas have entered the women's movement. This means that the women's movement cannot now avoid the challenge of situating itself within the global political and economic order. It must examine its own part in the processes of globalisation. In this, there is an important role for those involved in Women's Studies, not only in examining the impact of globalisation on women, but most importantly in reflecting critically upon the international implications of women's agendas within the context of widening global inequalities.

In what follows, I draw on various reports from women in developing as well as developed countries to identify key issues in the Beijing proceedings. I then move on to explore the 'gender agenda', considering firstly, the 'gender efficiency' approach consistent with the neoliberal development model pushed by the Group of Seven (G7) developed countries, and secondly, the liberal feminist 'empowerment' approach, consistent with the international agenda of political liberalisation currently pursued by Western governments. A critique of the 'gender agenda' is developed through reference to the US Women's Lobby, which provides a model of advocacy-based legal rights activism, and to the experiences of women's legal rights activism in Africa and of Chilean and Palestinian women's NGOs. Finally, I note some issues that this 'gender agenda' raises for Women's Studies not least the challenges of global dialogue and of renewing the links between women's activism and feminist debate.

Women on the world stage: perspectives from Beijing

Women's experiences over the last ten years or more, have been marked by quite contradictory trends (see Brenner, 1993). The pursuit of 'free market' economics over a sustained period has seen a deterioration in the conditions of the lives of many women. The costs of welfare have shifted increasingly from the state to the household whilst women's employment has grown on terms and conditions that are generally insecure. In parallel with this, women's issues are at last becoming mainstream with the implementation of anti-discrimination legislation and equal opportunities policies. Women are advancing up the ladders in management and the professions, including academia, and are increasingly entering political and public office.

At the same time, the women's movement in countries such as the US and Britain has become depoliticised, fragmented and institutionalised. But in many developing countries women's activism appears to be on the upsurge: in Africa (Mikell, 1995) and in India (Agnihotri and Mazumdar, 1995), women are protesting against draconian structural adjustment programmes (SAPs). Their demands are for a greater say in politics not only to press for women's issues but to push for policies promoting a wider social and economic development from which women as well as men will benefit. In the different context of China, rural women's informal self-help networks, providing support for productive activities, social and health issues, are on the increase (Zhang, 1994).

These conflicting experiences of women set the context for Beijing Women's Conference. It has been said of this that it was 'not so much a conference about women: more a women's conference about the state of the world' (Noeleen Heyzer, Unifem). The Forum itself brought together around 30,000 women from 185 different countries, demonstrating the international reach of women's issues. The POA adopted at the official UN Conference marked a significant shift from a narrow focus on gender specific issues such as family planning, income generation and education, to a global perspective affirming women's rights as human rights; condemning rape as a war crime; and calling for calculations of women's unpaid labour in national statistics thus bringing women into the frame of macro-economic analysis and policy-making.

Running through the conference proceedings was an emphasis on the need for women's greater participation in political processes. To set an example here, the UN, throughout the two years of preparation for the Conference, involved women's NGOs in the drafting of the POA. Many governments, including Britain's, also involved representatives from women's NGOs in their delegations to the official UN Conference itself.

The purpose of the Forum was 'to set an agenda for the women's movement throughout the world, to build networks among women in the North and South and to lobby the UN to turn the agendas of the NGO Forum into policy' (Report of the UK Delegation, 1995, p.81). With some 5,000 workshops and activities covering a tremendous range of issues, demonstrating the diverse concerns and energies of women, the Forum had a celebratory feel.

Irene Santiago, the Executive Director of the NGO Forum, opened the proceedings with no lack of boldness, stressing the need for 'solid analysis that identifies the root cause of problems and "names our enemies"' (ibid p.82). But who are the enemies? The views of the participants were so diverse: Christian and Islamic fundamentalist groups attacked others as godless, non-feminine and anti-family; there were conflicts over lesbian rights; the issue of 'Comfort Women' caused controversy between Korean and Japanese women; there was a silent vigil by Tibetan women in protest against human rights violations in China; there was even a very small pro-life march (ibid p.31; Magarey, 1995, p.146).

Nevertheless, Forum participants largely shared a view of the necessity to resist attempts by the conservative and fundamentalist lobby to roll back the agendas of women's reproductive and health rights. Nor did the melee of diversity obscure the widespread concern over the negative impact on women of SAPs forced on governments by the World Bank and International Monetary Fund (IMF). Delegates from developed as well as developing countries condemned the 'ascendancy of market ideology' and queried 'all talk of peace, equality and development which remained uncritical of the current trends of globalisation' (Agnihotri, 1995, p.3195).

But where the views of women in developed and developing countries did appear to diverge was with regard to the role of the NGOs and the extent of their influence on the official proceedings. Doub (1995), for example, writes positively of the NGOs' input into the drafting of the POA, emphasising their importance in turning 'grass roots concerns into UN policies' (ibid, p.80). Actually, the shaping of the POA had far more to do with the international political and economic agendas of Western governments. Asian Feminists were clearer in criticising the draft POA as 'an explicit endorsement of the current process of globalisation at the behest of the WB-IMF' (Agnihotri, 1995, p.3195; Raghuram and Manorama, 1995, p.2163).

At the Forum itself, many women from developing countries were also sceptical of the influence of First World based donor agencies in the selective accreditation of NGOs. Almost two-thirds of the 30,000 delegates were from the industrialised North - the US, Canada, Europe and Japan (Agnihotri, 1995, p.3195; Doub, 1995, p.81). At one point, mention of the donor agencies at a plenary session drew an angry cry from the floor: 'Funds to NGOs often don't reach the people they are supposed to help. They are thieves and robbers!' (Magarey, 1995, p.144).

Doub attributes the lack of success of the conservative Right - the Vatican, US Christian and Islamic fundamentalists to NGO 'assertiveness and well-organised advocacy' (ibid, p.86). But with the focus on women's rights and health issues, the negative effects of SAPs on women's lives, the issues of debt cancellation, and the regulation of the TNCs were insufficiently addressed. The sections of the POA regarding poverty and economic inequality remained weak (Beijing Forum UK Newsletter, No 3, p.3). So, in the final outcome, it was the agenda of the G7, which aimed to underscore the positive potential of market forces and SAPs, that prevailed over the concerns of developing countries.

Globalising liberal Feminism: economic liberalisation and 'gender efficiency'

It has often been stated that women do two-thirds of the world's work yet receive only 10% of the world's income and own a mere 1% of the world's wealth. The UNDP's 1995 Human Development Report now calls on governments to make gender disaggregated data available to give recognition to the importance of the women's role in the global economy. According to the report's author, Dr ul Huq, there is an 'unwitting conspiracy on a global scale to undervalue women's work and contribution to society'. Revealing how much women's work is worth in national accounts, he claims, will change women's status: 'it will shatter male society to see that women are actually the breadwinners' (Guardian, 18 August 1995).

The UNDP Report sets up a Gender Empowerment Measure to calculate women's participation in economic, political and professional activities, and a Gender-related Development Index to compare literacy, life expectancy and economic data. The lowest scorers in these league tables are in Africa and Asia whilst Scandinavian countries score the highest. This Scandinavian success, the Report maintains, shows how the 'gender gap' can be closed by means of legislation and quotas. It recommends that all countries implement the Convention to Eliminate Discrimination Against Women (CEDAW) within ten years.

Following the incorporation of the Report's recommendations into the POA, 'engendering human development' has become a priority. Development practitioners now set out to identify 'gender gaps' as the starting point for 'mainstreaming the gender perspective into all policies'. However, it is important to recognise that the UNDP's apparently radical departure here is consistent with what Razavi and Miller (1995) have identified as a pro-market 'gender efficiency' approach (ibid pp.18-27).

This approach, which uses neoliberal tools of analysis in conceptualising gender, has had some influence on international financial institutions. The World Bank, for example, now incorporates a gender perspective in its policies. The view is that discrimination causes high development costs since it distorts the allocation of resources, namely women's labour (see Stewart, 1996, p.28). Legislation against discrimination and equal opportunities policies is then advanced as a means to better resource utilisation.

'Gender efficiency' it may be argued, is an advance on previous development strategies which, whilst targeting aid to women, failed to consider how discriminatory practices might obstruct these efforts. It shifts the focus onto consideration of how gender biases and rigidities, that is, the structure of power relations between men and women affect and frustrate policy (Razavi and Miller, 1995, p.18). But the perspective is essentially instrumentalist in its approach towards women as agents of economic growth. Women's reproductive role is only considered to be of macro-economic relevance as an economic cost insofar as it constrains women's capacities to engage in productive activities (ibid, p.21). Patriarchal structures, institutions, customs and attitudes which discriminate against women for example, with regard to land ownership, divisions of labour, and control of finance and credit, are reviewed as barriers preventing the benefits of neoliberal policies from 'trickling down' to women, to be removed in order to allow market mechanisms to operate 'freely' (ibid, p.19).

In other words, the 'gender efficiency' approach accepts as fundamental that economic liberalisation is the best guarantee of prosperity and freedom, with the proviso that gender analysis is brought into the design of SAPs. The underlying economic logic here is for developing countries to promote a more rational use of women's labour in the production of cheap and competitive exports in order to repay their debts (ibid, p.20).

But clearly a feminist critique of macro-economics must extend beyond the issue of making women's unpaid labour visible. What needs to be addressed are the wider issues of global crisis which jeopardise the quality of women's lives - the increasing economic insecurities, the growing polarisation between the rich and the poor, of whom two-thirds are women, the privatisation of health care and education as well as the abuse of women's rights within environments of rising crime, violence and social disorder generated by policies of unequal growth.

However the obstacles that the 'gender efficiency' approach identifies are not the issues of debt, reductions in aid, the inequities of GATT, financial speculation and so forth, but patriarchal customs and attitudes per se. Yet how meaningful can it be to pursue policies of equal opportunity between men and women in developing countries without addressing the inequality of opportunity between North and South?

Globalising liberal Feminism: political liberalisation and the export of the model of the US Women's lobby

When Western donor agencies sent women NGO practitioners round the world - especially to Eastern Europe and to the developing countries - to train women in advocacy skills in preparation for the Beijing meeting, they certainly contributed to mobilising for the Forum. But they were also exporting a very particular form of women's political organisation: the model of the US Women's lobby. This liberal feminist model focuses on processes of legal and institutional reform rather than structural transformation, operating through methods of advocacy, networking, and training rather than mobilising the grass roots (Brenner, 1993).

Women organising to advocate for women are now a well-established part of the American political scene. No longer a movement of grass roots activists, the feminist movement is more of a professionalised and increasingly narrow network of experienced lobbyists pressing for legislative change. The wide vision of women's self-organisation and social transformation has given way to single-issue campaigns, and energies are directed more to fund-raising than organising collective action (ibid, pp.109-110; 118-122).

Liberal Feminism rests its moral claim on championing women's individual liberty against patriarchal power and privilege. It views the state not so much as a provider of welfare but as a regulator, ensuring free and fair competition, non-discrimination and individual freedom of choice. Brenner (1993) demonstrates how the US women's movement took on this individualistic ideology in order to capture the moral ground from the conservative Right particularly over the issue of abortion. Under pressure from anti-abortionists, Feminist arguments became narrowly focused on an individual's right to abort an unwanted pregnancy, that is, her right to decide her own private life (ibid, p.134). Liberal Feminism otherwise adopts much of the conservative agenda, viewing discrimination as a violation of market principles.

One example of how Western governments have adopted the model of the US Women's Lobby for export is provided in the speech given by Lady Chaulker at the UN Conference in Beijing. In this, she identified four main issues: mainstreaming a gender perspective into all policies; ensuring that all women, regardless of age, ethnicity, religion, disability or other characteristics, have equal opportunities, choices and rights; supporting women's promotion to the top of public and working life; and working in partnership with NGOs and others with an interest to take forward the objectives of the POA (Report of the UK Delegation, 1995, p. 26).

Her liberal democratic perspective is made transparent as she adds:

> If this Conference achieves only one thing it should be a global recognition of women's right to freedom of choice (her emphasis). Women must be

treated as individuals; we must respect and support their personal choices (ibid, p.26).

The approach here not only complements the pro-market rationale of 'gender efficiency' but also fits the wider political agenda of reforming states along liberal democratic lines. This agenda has been actively pursued by Western governments and international agencies through policies linking aid, trade and investment to political changes emphasising good governance, human rights and the rule of law. The UNDP has again played a part in this with its loose definition of 'democratisation' - the right to vote together with a wide range of civil rights - included in the Human Development Index.

In response to concerns about the human costs of unfettered market competition, this political agenda claims legitimacy for neoliberal economic orthodoxy by making the connection between open markets and intellectual and political liberties and human rights. Such claims derive from a particular view of the Western experience of the rise of capitalism which conceives the growth of the market as intrinsically associated with the rise of individualism, the rule of law, progress toward freedom and the autonomy of civil society. Accordingly, state corruption and abuse of law, and costly bureaucracy, together with economic intervention by the state, are identified as the main obstacles to efficiency, and hence, in neoliberal terms, to development. A strong civil society, that is, individual freedom of association and independent activity, pluralism and diversity, is valued as essential in limiting the coercive impositions of the state. Electoral politics and legal institutions provide the chief means to do so.

That the assumptions here derive from an idealised view of Western history is evidenced not least by the campaigns for women's suffrage. Clearly civil rights were extended only gradually, and then won through struggle.

Women's rights are human rights - but what are human rights?

As the result of struggles against colonial rule and for national liberation, states in many parts of the Third World have rested their legitimacy on the goals of independence and development. Women across Asia, Africa, the Middle East and Latin America were integrally involved in these struggles for independence and for economic and social reconstruction; their organisations became actively involved in state-building and women gained many rights. As women's equal rights in marriage, inheritance and suffrage were written into the new constitutions, the legitimacy of many independent states was also seen to rest on their role as a modernising progressive force against traditional patriarchal practices. Relations between state and society therefore took on a different dynamic from the individual-versus-state conception of the liberal democratic paradigm.

Nonetheless, after decolonisation, Feminist agendas often became subsumed by the nationalist cause. More recently, where states have turned back to tradition to shore up their legitimacy as development plans falter, nationalism and Feminism have come into conflict. These conflicts have been complicated all the more by the West's vigorous global pursuit of its liberal agendas.

In Africa, where aid has been attached to conditions of good governance and the promotion of legal rights, with the aim of undermining customary practices and corrupt governments, pressures to develop a strong legal system are seen as a form of external interference, and in turn, the defence of custom and tradition has become a form of resistance. In these circumstances, women's legal rights activism has proved highly problematic (Stewart, 1996). Women who attempt to enforce their rights through the courts may be championed by international agencies but often find themselves regarded by their compatriots as anti-African, in unholy alliance not only with Western feminists but also with international bodies responsible for draconian economic policies (ibid, pp.29, 39).

In Asia, similar conflicts have been apparent. Whilst some states have adopted a position of cultural relativism in reaction against pressures from Western governments calling for political freedoms and human rights, this stance has not been acceptable to some Asian Feminists who consider that customary patriarchal practices can be extremely harmful to women (Khan et al, 1995, p.8-9; Agnihotri, 1995, p.3196).

This does not mean that Feminists in Africa and Asian ignore the existence of cultural differences. On the contrary, seeking ways to avoid a contest between tradition and Feminism, African women researchers have suggested that traditional forms of conflict resolution may be a more successful method of tackling male power in the African countryside than working through the Westernised processes of the modern legal system. In their view 'the customary is best seen as processal rather than substantive' (Stewart, p.40). In other words, whilst the struggle for women's rights has a universal content, it is the forms which these struggles take that may be relative to cultural context.

The difficulty in universalising women's rights as human rights is not simply about cultural or national difference: the problem is primarily that of defining human rights themselves. Whilst the POA marked a shift from a recognition of women's special needs to an affirmation of women's rights as human rights it begs the questions: what are women's rights? What are human rights?

Take, for example, the definition of reproductive rights. Liberal Feminists in the US have claimed the right to abortion is an individual freedom. Black Women's organisations, on the other hand, emphasise the need to link women's right to control over their own bodies to a broader set of social rights including affordable contraception and abortion and universal health care (Brenner, pp.130-137). Women from developing countries have similarly opposed a narrow emphasis on family planning which ignores women's health needs, arguing for a conception of reproductive rights within a wider programme of women's health care.

This debate reflects different approaches towards human rights as an issue of individual or collective concern. Western liberal democracy emphasises civil rights and individual and political freedoms. But should human rights encompass more than this? Should they also include social rights such as education, health and not least the fundamental right to subsistence - rights associated with the fulfilment of human potential to develop? Both social and civil rights are in fact included in the Universal Declaration of Human Rights adopted by the UN in 1948.

In the Western capitalist system the division of the political and the economic spheres permits liberal democratic states to claim legitimacy in terms of the universality of citizenship, that is, the equal distribution of civil rights, whilst maintaining an unequal distribution of economic power and social goods. Such a separation of civil and social rights is not so easily acceptable in developing countries where popular mandate rests on the goals of stability and development.

According to the Western liberal agenda, of course, democratic rights and an active civil society are the means to development. But this is a claim which is yet to be proved. Taylor's recent study of 18 examples of SAPs in developing countries has shown, on the contrary, that directed intervention and 'hands-on management' by authoritarian states have achieved better economic results than policies of wholesale economic liberalisation which might even run the risk of economic collapse (Taylor, 1988, p.168).

In East Asia, authoritarian states have maintained stability, playing a developmental role in achieving high rates of economic growth. This has seen, in some cases more than others, a general improvement in social conditions which have not been entirely without social and economic benefit for women (Lim, 1990, pp.108-119). In contrast, in the former Soviet Union and Eastern Europe, the 'triumph' of civil society against the state and freedom for the individual has seen a massive shift of wealth into the hands of a small minority.

Rather than democracy leading to development, many developing countries are experiencing difficulties in building democracy in conditions of inequity and social disorder generated by the imposition of neoliberal economic policies of the IMF and the World Bank.

These trends all raise significant challenges for Feminist analyses of the Third World state (Rai, 1996) as well as dilemmas for Women's organisations in developing countries in formulating strategies for gaining civil and social rights. Political and legal reforms carried out to remove the 'obstacles' of the state above and customary practices below may leave many women worse off. Especially in rural areas, in the absence of alternative opportunities, local communities and households often cling to subsistence strategies and traditional arrangements of land and labour as a defence against the disruption and often devastating impact of commercialism and market competition.

The value of a legal system and electoral politics is not to be denied. But clearly in conditions of poverty and illiteracy, these systems have their limits. Rather than democratic rights and civil liberties preceding development, legislation and election systems can really only be strengthened as part of a development process which promotes social conditions enabling the broad population to use the law and exercise their vote. So it is essentially within a wider context of national development that anti-discrimination and legal rights activism can facilitate women's social and economic development. The progressive strengthening of women's organisations as institutions of a civil society may then be better achieved step-by-step, within the limits of a programme of economic development with a commitment to social rights.

The role of women's NGOs

The West's agenda of good governance and democratisation gives much attention to the role of NGOs as playing a vital part in promoting citizenry and facilitating the emergence of a strong civil society. The weight given to NGOs by government delegations at the UN Women's Conference takes on a particular significance in this context.

To British women participants at Beijing, this emphasis on the role of NGOs was the most important breakthrough at the Conference. Women who, ten years ago at the UN Women's Conference in Nairobi, were demonstrating *against* the UK delegation, were now *included as members of* the delegation. To these NGO practitioners, researchers and academics, gaining recognition in the international arena for their expertise and professionalism, for their roles in lobbying and networking, is more than a personal victory. It represents a much wider shift towards recognition of gender as a power relation, conferring empowerment to women away from those who seek power over them.

In seeking to 'mainstream gender' into policy-making arenas and decision-making processes, Feminists have tended to conceive the institutions of the state and civil society simply in terms of male domination. Yet what also complicates the relations between civil society and the state is that both are also sites of class divisions. In developing countries, the interaction of gender and national interests provides a further complex dynamic. Empowerment in this context does not mean simply 'men giving up power': women as well as men may be empowered through the pursuit of national goals of independence and economic and social development set against international domination.

In identifying a positive role for women's NGOs in development, Young, (1993) makes an important distinction between individual empowerment, in the sense of unleashing an individual's entrepreneurial capacities - 'getting women into the cash economy' - and collective empowerment, involving the transformation of processes and structures which reproduce women's subordination as women (ibid, pp.158-9). She sees NGOs in the second sense as having a role as catalysts, bringing together groups such as women and the rural poor who are otherwise marginalised from formal institutions, creating spaces for them to articulate their demands.

This emphasis on the collective empowerment of the poor clearly distinguishes Young from the pro-market 'gender efficiency' approach (Razavi and Miller, 1995, p.35). Yet whilst acknowledging that structures of power have a complex national and class as well as a gendered nature, Young's analysis ultimately discounts international agendas from the power equation, when she refers positively to the 'posture of Western governments and international agencies such as the World Bank on good governance' as potentially creating spaces within political culture to allow women's pressure groups to influence state policies (Young, 1993, p.161). This Western stand may also apparently encourage governments to 'empower' by supporting NGOs and using them as consultative bodies (ibid, p.163). Young's arguments rest on the aspiration that democratisation processes open up a path to the more equitable restructuring of gender and class relations. But what in practice has been the role of women's NGOs in democratisation and development?

Two cases studies from the developing world

The Chilean experience : In Latin America during the 1970s numerous women's organisations emerged, mobilising in opposition to authoritarian regimes across the sub-continent. Within a few years, international funding began to pour in to support local initiatives with the purpose of fostering a democratic opposition (Schild, 1995, pp.132-133). By the 1990s, the movement was marked by deep fragmentation and demobilisation. Schild's study (1995) of women's NGOs in Chile brings this transformation into focus, identifying a shift from the collective goals of feminist activists to an emphasis on women's empowerment in terms of access to resources and individual choice in line with neoliberal ideology. This shift came about as the context in which women organised completely altered as a result of the change to a liberal democratic government in 1990 and with a new emphasis in international agendas on open markets and private ownership, with NGOs designated a new role in creating an 'enabling environment' of self-help. Whilst international donor agencies tightened their funding criteria, the government set up a national body, SERNAM (*Servicio Nacional de la Mujer*), to oversee social policies and programmes affecting women. There have been legislative gains with regard to divorce and property rights, but, Schild argues, SERNAM's work depends increasingly on a network of women professionals (ibid, p.141). As NGOs 'retool' under more tightly controlled conditions, those organisations which originated among the middle classes have been able to survive through co-option whilst organisations at the local and community level which originated among the poor and working class, have had the most difficultly in adjusting (ibid, pp.136-137). Groups organised around popular education and movement building have been overtaken by service-providing NGOs.

The Palestinian experience

Women's organisations flourished during the Palestinian *intifada* as women became active participants in the wider struggle to end Israeli occupation and create an independent Palestinian state (Abdo, 1991). Organisation during this period concentrated on the broader question of women's participation in the development process as women took part in handicraft production projects both as an alternative to Israeli goods and to increase their own economic independence and social participation (Holt, 1996, pp.68-69). This activism stands in contrast to the present situation in which NGOs have become increasingly isolated from the grass roots communities. Hammami's analysis (1995) of this trend refers to a number of factors: the involvement of international donor agencies in the increasing professionalisation of the NGOs, the Israeli suppression of any popular organisation, and the ideological confusion within Palestinian political parties following the signing of the Oslo accords and also the fall of the USSR (ibid, pp.57-68). As the political movement has disintegrated and factionalised under ideological discord, the Women's Movement itself has split along religious as well as political lines (Holt, 1996, p.71).

NGOs and politics

NGOs are undoubtedly encouraged by Western governments and international donor agencies to see themselves in the forefront of democratisation, as a progressive force for justice and individual empowerment. But from the experiences above, it can be seen that a more critical examination of their role is called for. Who, and what, do the NGOs represent?

Clearly NGOs are very diverse both in size and aims, encompassing local, national and international organisations. They have often grown out of grass roots activism as part of a wider political movement. But this means that the distinction between grassroots organisations and officially registered NGOs is easily blurred even as the latter become increasingly separated and isolated from their roots and more dependent on international funding.

NGOs frequently face problems of lack of client participation, of conflicts among clients, of mismatch between the clients' perceptions of their needs and the outcomes required by the donor organisations. It is however, only a short step.for NGOs to take from advocacy and lobbying to substituting themselves 'for the masses'. In some instances NGOs are forming themselves into political organisations to take an active part in electoral politics (Hammami, 1995, pp.60-61). But there is a big difference between the development practice of NGOs and mass-based political parties; between the provision of a service to meet clients' needs, and the political debate necessary to form an agenda with mass appeal; between the manifestos of political organisations and the measurable outcomes of NGO work designed to meet the guidelines of the donor agencies.

As the energies of activists are absorbed into fund-raising, NGOs have a depoliticising effect (Khan, 1995, p.333). Schild goes further in identifying the repositioning of women, some as clients and others as advocates, as a move towards the creation of class-based hierarchies (Schild, 1995, p.143). Such developments are achieved increasingly through the support of international donor agencies which may also promote the potential for NGOs to circumvent national governments: it is striking, for example, that the Indian government, in the preparations for the Beijing NGO Forum, could only deal with its own NGOs through the mediation of a donor-established co-ordinating bureau (Agnihotri, 1995, p.3198). Operating within the constraints of their funders' guidelines, NGOs may rather serve as vehicles for Western advice than agents of grass roots democratisation.

Such trends call for Feminist analyses to extend beyond generalisations about 'collective empowerment'. It is important to recognise that what can be achieved by women's collective action is conditioned by the wider, political context - the strength of grass roots activism, the capacities of political parties to address people's needs on a sustained basis and the strategies and responses of states and international agencies. Concrete political analysis is all the more important in locating women's organisations within the global context given that the current emphasis on NGOs as agents of democratisation is but one strand of an international agenda aimed at widening class differentials and limiting the defences of the nation-state against the demands of economic globalisation.

The 'gender agenda': a hidden agenda?

The 'gender agenda' promoted by Western Governments at the UN Conference and in the preparations leading up to it, in their consultations with NGOs, may be seen to have the following logic:

(a) *Gender efficiency*: women's labour, skills and abilities are to be put to the most efficient economic use by 'freeing the market';

(b) *Anti-discrimination legislation:* ensuring the efficient allocation of women's labour by using the legal process against such obstacles to the market mechanism as government corruption (nepotism), bureaucratic interference (discrimination), patriarchal customs and traditions regarding, for example, the use of land, and the division of labour;

(c) *Legal activism and the advocacy role of NGOs*: lobbying for legal reforms to abolish discrimination; empowering women to use these laws to remove patriarchal and bureaucratic barriers;

(d) *Women's political representation*: women's participation in electoral politics to carry through the legislation, and their recruitment into organisations such as the IMF, WB and UN, as well as governments, to ensure that gender issues are built into national and global policies.

Whilst this strategy claims to provide a new form of response to the negative impact of globalisation, it is hard to see this 'engendering of human development' other than as an endeavour to provide the prevailing neoliberal economic order with a humanitarian face. The dominance of liberal Feminism within the US women's movement does indeed provide an object lesson here: as Brenner's analysis (1993) so clearly highlights, the shift from activism to advocacy, which took place as the movement became increasingly depoliticised and fragmented occurred in parallel with a deterioration in conditions for the majority of women, and the increasing polarisation between their experiences and those of the minority of women professionals.

A meaningful agenda for women should identify the ways in which the neoliberal orthodoxy of the IMF and WB has worsened conditions for the majority of women. But in 'naming the enemies', liberal Feminism deflects focus from the agenda of the G7 onto the patriarchal customs and the authoritarian states in the Third World with their poor records of individual human rights and civil liberties. As criticisms of the Chinese government's organisation of the Women's NGO Forum added to the much-publicised list of China's abuses of women's and human rights, many Western Feminists doubtless felt that they were taking the message to the place where it was most needed. However, for one Indian Feminist at least, this singling out of China was part of a politically motivated strategy: abuses of women occur all over the world, in developed as well as developing countries, under liberal democratic as well as authoritarian states (Agnihotri, 1995, p.3195).

Developing countries are often seen to experience the most extreme forms of patriarchal oppression. Women are regarded as victims suffering the most brutal abuses of their rights and freedoms as individuals: female infanticide, bride burning, girl prostitution. If the abuses of women are viewed simply through the prism of individual rights, globalisation may appear to have a positive potential insofar as commercialisation sweeps away patriarchal traditions and undermines the male-dominated institutions of coercive states. But for women in developing countries, who see their deteriorating conditions in the context of the general social crisis brought about at the behest of international capitalism, collective organisation remains the most effective response.

With its emphasis on training in advocacy and other 'democratic' practices, the effect of the 'gender agenda' is to supplant agendas of collective action. It is often argued that it is difficult to organise women as women, since women have multiple identities of class, ethnicity, age and so on. However, the problem is not in organising women as such. The difficulties in mobilising women tend to be perceived from the viewpoint of NGOs, in terms of development, rather than political, practice. In fact, the organisational capacities of the NGOs are limited: their approach is that of organising women *separately*. It is only within the context of wider social movements that women begin to articulate what they want. The issue for collective organisation here is that of women's *autonomy* - to ensure their demands are carried forward within an overall political perspective.

The Women's Movement in India provides a current example as it experiences an upsurge from the grass roots in response to the destructive impact of structural adjustment on the Indian economy, and especially on the lives of women (Agnihotri and Mazumdar, 1995). As women's organisations have drawn together in opposition to GATT and the unrestricted entry of TNCs, unity among the different strands of the women's movement has been easier to achieve. In a joint statement, women's organisations asserted: 'In our multidimensional roles, as workers, as peasants, as producers, as citizens as mothers, wives, daughters, as women, the economic policies hit us the hardest' (ibid, p.1876). This widespread upsurge is even occurring in states where women have previously not been active.

Some issues for Women's Studies

This discussion has aimed to emphasis that the women's movement needs now to be able to situate itself within the wider trends of globalisation, and to examine the relevance of the international political context in framing agendas for women. This is a challenge in which Feminist academics, as researchers, analysts and teachers, can play a valuable role.

But critical analysis of women's agendas also requires that the critics reflect upon their own roles. We may celebrate the diversity of women's energies displayed at the Beijing Forum, but it must be recognised that the 'global sisterhood' is becoming more divided as gaps widen between and within nations, between rich and poor, between urban and rural. It must also be seen how 'mainstreaming gender' can be a part of these processes, reinforcing divisions between the professionals, the advocates, those with access to the networks of new technologies on the one hand, and the illiterate, the poor, the clients, on the other.

As women's movements have become institutionalised, and Women's Studies itself has become recognised as an academic discipline, Feminist scholarship has increasingly taken on board the perspectives of planners and policy practitioners. But with the movement now entering onto the world stage, it is all the more important to seek to renew the links between Feminist research and women's collective activism.

International networking is clearly of value but there is the question of how to engage in dialogue which extends beyond the new global elites served by the Internet. At the very least, global dialogue cannot develop on an assumption that Feminist ideas just 'trickle down' from the writings of Betty Friedan. Women's movements in developing countries have long histories rooted in anti-colonial and democratic struggles. In India, for example, the women's movement consists of many different local, national, single issue, mass organisations, some with 50 and 100 year histories (Agnihotri and Mazumdar, 1995, p.1876). Women's Studies programmes are also flourishing across Africa, Asia and Latin America often connected with women's research centres. As these Feminist activists and researchers seek to rediscover their own women's histories and re-evaluate their cultures and religions, their perspectives contribute to the search for new forms of Feminist legitimacy which extend definitions of women's rights as human rights beyond the terms of capitalist economy, namely, access to resources and individual freedom of choice, by bringing Feminist debate back to its core: the issue of women's self-determination (Khan et al, 1995, pp.ii-iii).

A last point: it is also clearly important to include courses with an international perspective in the Women's Studies curriculum and to 'create spaces' for women and men to reflect upon the options for women within a world frame, developing a 'global sense' of their own situation within the processes which generate the growing gaps between women.

15 Conclusion

Fiona Montgomery and Christine Collette

There can be no doubt that Women's Studies/Feminism has influenced mainstream academic life. Not only are Women's Studies courses established in their own right but the influence on other disciplines such as Geography, Drama, Communication Studies, Afro-Asian Studies, is accepted, albeit sometimes unwillingly, within the academy. Nevertheless, Women's Studies courses are impossibly, vulnerably, new in relation to other disciplines. One deeply unfortunate aspect of this fragility has been experienced during the preparation of this book. Two of our contributors have been adversely affected by 'downsizing', a potential problem we have noted in discussing the operation of a market philosophy in academia. This can be seen as part of a general back-lash against not only Feminists but also women in general. Such a trend affects both us as teachers and also our students; our contributors have remarked upon the local/community aspect of Women's Studies. Thus, students now often come from an environment where Women's Studies' ideals are not commonly accepted, which impacts upon their project work and approach to their studies. This is a change from the academic history described by Kelly, Burton and Regan (1994, p.28), who wrote that 1970s and 1980s academic work could be read as 'a story in which differences between women were sometimes recognised and where conflicts and struggles about race, class and sexuality were commonplace within Feminist groups, campaigns and organisations'. In this position of vulnerability, we must continue to defend Women's Studies, which involves refining its practice and philosophy.

Part of the influence of Women's Studies comes from its undoubted contribution to progressive pedagogy. Women's Studies pedagogy has developed because Feminist lecturers have experimented, conferred, debated, dared to invent and imagine an alternative to the traditional academic experience for both teacher and student. This has happened simultaneously across the different education strata. Of what does this Women's Studies pedagogy consist? It is student centred; it reflects upon the relationship between the student and the teacher; it aims to engage all students, in a highly participative way; it values honesty in teaching. In detail, this means group work, presentations and self assessment. All of this makes the teacher vulnerable. No longer is it possible to rely on the certainty of oneself as the fount of all knowledge; indeed, Women's Studies teachers purposely undermine themselves as keepers of wisdom.

It may be asked how Women's Studies' teaching differs from progressive pedagogy *per se*? The answer, of course, lies in the Feminist philosophy which informs it; so Women's Studies pedagogy is progressive, but not all progressive pedagogy is Feminist. It is clear that the philosophy of Women's Studies is still emerging, and this is part of the discipline's vibrancy. As Philomena Harrison, Sneh Shah and Jenny Clegg have shown, it will be crucial to advocate strongly the Black and post-Colonial critique of Eurocentrism and ethnocentrism in the White Feminist discourse. How women work together across organisations, issues of power, authority, leadership are areas which demand the attention of Feminists.

Having challenged the idea that Women's Studies as an academic discipline had little of relevance to the 'ordinary' woman's life, Beryl Madoc Jones has shown that both lecturers and students are 'ordinary' women who bring their experiences to the classroom and are often affected by what happens there. Women's Studies must continue to provide a safe area from which to mount resistance to and assaults upon systems of oppression. For this reason we are determined that our discipline should continue to be called 'Women's Studies', not 'Gender Studies', because we do not want to lose the ground we have won; to hide or apologise for Women's Studies. Under the umbrella of another discipline, such as Sociology, Women's Studies disappears. The honesty which we prize must not be undermined. As Professor Mary Evans says: 'Women's Studies have always been about relationships. Gender studies is either just a code for a rethought sociology where women have been fitted in or another term for gay studies' (*Guardian*, 25 March 1997). An example of this was the 1996 Research Assessment Exercise (RAE); here, much Women's Studies work was hidden in Social Sciences, Humanities or Education submissions because there was no category 'Women's Studies'. This means that established (often male) academics gain credit and the consequent funding.

These chapters have demonstrated that Women's Studies practitioners need to continue attacking gender stereotypes and to construct a new Feminist praxis. Women's Studies in the new millennium, therefore, will continue to deal with the transformative power of Feminism and the ways in which it promotes alternative ways of thinking and shifts boundaries; it will engage with the product of the present *Melting Pot*.

Bibliography

Aaron, J. and Walby, S. (eds.), (1991), *Out of the Margins: Women's Studies in the Nineties,* Falmer Press: London.
Abdo, N. (1991), 'Women of the Intifada: Gender, Class and National Liberation', *Race and Class*, Vol.32, No.4, April-June, pp.19-34.
Abel, K. et al. (eds.), (1996), *Planning Community Mental Health Services for Women, A Multiprofessional Handbook,* Routledge: London.
Acker, S. (1994), *Gendered Education: Sociological Reflections on Women, Teaching and Feminism*, Open University Press: Buckingham.
Afshar, H. and Maynard, M. (1994), *The Dynamics of 'Race' and 'Gender': Some Feminist Interventions*, Taylor and Francis: London.
Agnihotri, I. (1995), 'Evolving a Women's Agenda: Report from Beijing', *Economic and Political Weekly*, Vol.XXX, No. 50, pp.3195-9.
Agnihotri, I. and Mazumdar, V. (1995), 'Changing the Terms of Political Discourse: Women's Movement in India, 1970s-1990s', *Economic and Political Weekly*, Vol.XXX, No. 29, pp.1869-78.
Ang, I. (1989), *Watching Dallas,* Hutchinson: London.
Ang, I. (1991), *Desperately Seeking the Audience*, Routledge: London.
Ang, I. and Hermes, J. (1988), 'Gender and/in Media Consumption' in Curran, J. and Gurevitch, M. (eds.), *Mass Media and Society*, Edward Arnold: London.
Atkinson, J. (1992), 'How are Women in the Third World Portrayed in Geography Textbooks?', *Teaching Geography,* Vol.17, pp.179-80.
Barrett, M. and Philips, A. (eds.), (1992), *Destabilising Theory: Contemporary Feminist Debate,* Polity Press: London.
Belenky, M. (1986), *Ways of Knowing: the Development of Self*, Basic Books: London and New York.
Bell, D. and Valentine, G. (eds.), (1995), *Mapping Desire*, Routledge: London.
Bhavnani, K., Phoenix, A. (eds.), (1994), *Shifting Identities, Shifting Racisms*, Sage Publications: London.

Bignell, K.C. (1996), 'Building Feminist Praxis out of Feminist Pedagogy: the Importance of Students' Perspectives', *Women's Studies International Forum,* Vol.19, No.3. pp.315-325.

Binder, E. (1989), 'Feminist Geography in Austria, Switzerland and Germany', *Journal of Geography in Higher Education,* Vol.13, pp.97-9.

Bird, L. (1980), 'Setting up.Women's Studies Courses', *Spare Rib,* No. 93, pp.52-53.

Bondi, L. and Peake, L. (1988), 'Fending for Ourselves: Women as Teachers of Geography in Higher Education', *Journal of Geography in Higher Education,* Vol.12, pp.216-8.

Bowlby, S. (1989), 'The Development of Feminist Geography in Britain', *Journal of Geography in Higher Education,* Vol.13, pp.90-2.

Bowlby, S. (1992), 'Feminist Geography and the Changing Curriculum', *Geography,* Vol.77, pp.349-60.

Bowlby, S., Foord, J. and MacKenzie, S. (1982), 'Feminism and Geography', *Area,* Vol.14, pp.19-25.

Bowlby, S. and McDowell, L. (1986), 'The Feminist Challenge to Social Geography' in Pacione, M. (ed.), *Progress in Social Geography,* Croom Helm: Sussex.

Bowles, G. and Duelli Klein, R. (eds.), (1983), *Theories of Women's Studies,* Routledge and Kegan Paul: London.

Brenner, J. (1993), 'The Best of Times, the Worst of Times: US Feminism Today', *New Left Review,* Issue 200, July/August, pp.101-59.

Brunsdon, C. (ed.), (1986), *Films for Women,* British Film Institute: London.

Bryan, B., Dadzie, S. and Scafe, S. (1985), *The Heart of the Matter,* Virago: London.

Calio, S.A. (1989), 'Feminist Geography in Brazil', *Journal of Geography in Higher Education,* Vol.13, p.89.

Cannon, L.W. (1990), 'Fostering Positive Race, Class and Gender Dynamics in the Classroom' ,*Women's Studies Quarterly,* Nos. 1 and 2.

Carby, H. (1982), 'White Women Listen!, Black Feminism and the Boundaries of Sisterhood', in Centre for Contemporary Studies, *The Empire Strikes Back,* Hutchinson: London, pp.212-36.

Carlen, P. (1983), *The Imprisonment of Women: A Study in Social Control.* Routledge: London.

Carlen, P. (1994), 'Why Study Women's Imprisonment, or Anyone Else's?' *Sociology Review,* Vol.1, pp.353-64.

Chernin, K. (1983), *Womansize, The Tyranny of Slenderness,* The Women's Press Ltd: London.

Chiang, N. (1989), 'Feminist Geography in Taiwan', *Journal of Geography in Higher Education,* Vol.13, pp.94-6.

Code, L. (1989), 'Experience, Knowledge and Responsibility' in Pearsall G. A. and M. (eds.), *Women, Knowledge and Reality,* Unwin Hyman: Boston.

Cohen, S. and Taylor, L. (1977), 'Talking about Prison Blues' in Bell, C. and Newby, H. (eds.), *Doing Sociological Research*, Allen and Unwin: London.
Connelly, C. (1990), 'Anti-racism', *Feminist Review*, No. 36, Autumn, pp.52-63.
Connolly, J. (1993), 'Gender Balanced Geography: Have We Got It Right Yet?' *Teaching Geography*, Vol.18, pp.61-4.
Corner, J. (ed.), (1991), *Popular Television in Britain: Studies in Cultural History*, British Film Institute: London.
Currie, D. and Kazi, H. (1987), 'Academic Feminism and the Process of De-radicalisation: Re-examining the Issues', *Feminist Review*, No. 25, pp.77-98.
Davis, A. (1981), *Women, Race and Class*, The Women's Press: London.
Department of Education and Science (1985), *Education for All* (Swann Report) HMSO: London.
Dill, B. (1994), 'Race, Class and Gender: Prospects for an All-Inclusive Sisterhood', in Stone, L. (ed.), *The Education Feminism Reader*, Routledge: London and New York, pp. 42-56.
Doub, M. (1995), 'Reflections on the NGO Forum on Women '95, *Bulletin of Concerned Asian Scholars*, Vol. 33, No. 3, pp. 80-8.
Editorial (1984), 'Geography in the Wilderness', *Teaching Geography*, Vol.9, pp.146-7.
Edney, M. and Langton, T. (1974), 'Feminist Subversion' *Spare Rib*, No. 20, pp.12-14.
Entwistle, N. (1992), *The Impact of Teaching on Learning Outcomes in Higher Education*, USDU, CVCP.
Essed, P. (1991), *Understanding Everyday Racism - an Interdisciplinary Theory*, Sage Publications: London.
Essed, P. (1994), 'Making and Breaking Ethnic Boundaries: Women's Studies, Diversity and Racism', *Women's Studies Quarterly*, Vol.22, Nos.3 and 4, pp.232-249.
Evans, M. (1982), 'In Praise of Theory: the Case for Women's Studies', *Feminist Review* No. 10, February, pp. 61-74.
Featherston, E. (ed.), (1994), *Skin Deep - Women Writing on Color, Culture and Identity*, The Crossing Press: Freedom, USA.
Fincher, R. (1989), 'Class and Gender Relations in the Local Labour Market and the Local State' in Wolch, J. and Dear, M. (eds.), *The Power of Geography*, Unwin Hyman: Boston.
Fiske, J. (1987), *Television Culture*, Methuen: London and New York.
Flax, J. (1990), 'Postmodernism and Gender Relations', in Nicholson, L.S. (ed.), *Feminism/Postmodernism*, Routledge: London.
Fonow, M.M. and Cook, J.A. (1991*)*, *Beyond Methodology: Feminist Scholarship as Lived Research*, Indiana University Press: Bloomington and Indianapolis.
Foord, J. and Gregson, N. (1986), 'Patriarchy: Towards a Reconceptualisation', *Antipode* Vol.18, pp.186-211.
Foord, J. (1980), 'Women's Place - Women's Space', *Area*, Vol.12, pp.49-50.

Foucault, M. (1977), *Discipline and Punish: The Birth of the Modern Prison*, Penguin: London.

Frankenberg, R. (1993), 'Growing Up White: Feminism, Racism and the Social Geography of Childhood', *Feminist Review*, No. 45, Autumn, pp.51-84.

Frankenburg, R. (1993), *The Social Construction of Whiteness, White Women, Race Matters,* Routledge: London.

Frazer, M. and Nicholson, L.J. (1990), 'Social Criticism without Philosophy' in Nicholson, L. (ed.), *An Encounter between Feminism and Postmodernism*, Routledge: London and New York.

Freire, P. (1972), *Pedagogy of the Oppressed,* Penguin Books: London.

Friedan, B. (1993), *The Feminine Mystique*, Pelican: London.

Fuss, D. (1990), 'Essentialism in the Classroom', in *Essentially Speaking: Feminism, Nature and Difference*, Routledge: London.

Gamman, L. and Marshment, M. (1988), *The Female Gaze*, The Women's Press: London.

Gelsthorpe, L. and Morris, A. (eds.), (1990), *Feminist Perspectives in Criminology*, Open University Press: Buckingham.

Genders, L. and Player, S. (1987), *Race Relations in Prisons*, Sage: London,

Gilligan, C. (1982), *In a Different Voice*, Harvard University Press: Cambridge, MA, and London.

Gontarczyk-Wesola, E. (1995), 'Towards a Space of Our Own: Feminist Research and Teaching in the Social Sciences', in *Women's Studies International Forum*, Vol.18 (1).

Gore, J.M. (1993), *The Struggle for Pedagogies: Critical and Feminist Discourses as Regimes Of Truth,* Routledge: London and New York.

Greed, C. (1993), 'The Professional and the Personal' in Stanley, L, *Feminist Praxis*, London and New York, Routledge: London.

Greer, G. (1970), *The Female Eunuch*, Macgibbon and Kee: London.

Haggett, P. (1972), (1979), *Geography: A Modern Synthesis*, Harper and Row: New York.

Hammami, R. (1995), 'NGOs: the Professionalisation of Politics', *Race and Class*, Vol.37, No.2, Oct-Dec, pp. 51-63.

Hanson, S. and Pratt, G. (1995), *Gender, Work and Space*, Routledge: London.

Harris, H.W. (1995), *Racial and Ethnic Identity - Psychological Development and Creative Expression*, Routledge: London.

Haskell, M. (1973), *From Reverence to Rape: The Treatment of Women in the Movies*, Penguin: London.

Higher Education Funding Council for England, Circular 3/94, *Continuing Education,* January, 1994.

Hill Collins, P. (1990), *Black Feminist Thought*, Routledge: London.

Hill, R. (1996), 'Women and Transport' in Booth, C., Warhe, J. and Yeande, S. (eds.), *Changing Places: Women's Lives in the City*, Paul Chapman Publishing: London.

Hobson, D. (1982), *Crossroads: The Drama of a Soap Opera*, Methuen: London.

Holloway, G. (1994), 'All Change: Accreditation and "Other" Learners' in Stuart, M. and Thomson, A. (eds.), *Engaging with Difference: The Other in Education*, Leicester, NIACE.

Holloway, G. (ed.), (1994), *All Change! Accreditations as a Challenge to Liberal Adult Education*, University of Sussex.

Holt, M. (1996), 'State-Building in the Absence of State Structures: Palestinian Women in the Occupied Territories and Shi'i Women in Lebanon', in Rai, S. and Lievesley, G.M. (eds.), *Women and the State: International Perspectives*, Taylor and Francis: London.

hooks, b. (1982, 1990) *Ain't I a Woman -Black Women and Feminism*, Pluto Press: London.

hooks, b. (1989), *Talking Back: Thinking Feminist, Thinking Black*, Sheba: London.

hooks, b. (1990), 'Sisterhood: Political Solidarity Between Women', in Gunew, S. (ed.), *Feminist Knowledge: Critique and Construct*, Routledge: London.

hooks, b. (1992), *Black Looks - Race and Representation*, Turnaround: London.

hooks, b. (1993), *Sisters of the Yam - Black Women and Self-Recovery*, Turnaround: London.

hooks, b. (1994), *Teaching to Transgress - Education as the Practice of Freedom*, Routledge: New York, London.

hooks, b. (1996), 'Sisterhood: Beyond Public and Private,' In *Signs*, Vol.21, No.4, pp. 814-829.

Humm, M. (1991), 'Thinking of Things in Themselves: Theory, Experience and Women's Studies', in Aaron, J. and Walby, S. (eds.), *Out of the Margins*, Falmer Press: London.

James, S.M. and Busia, A.P.A. (eds.), (1993), *Theorising Black Feminisms - the Visionary Pragmatism of Black Women*, Routledge: London.

Jarrett-Macauley, D. (ed.), (1996), *Reconstructing Womanhood, Reconstructing Feminism -Writings on Black Women*, Routledge: London.

Johnson, L.C. (1989), 'Feminist or Gender Geography in Australasia?', *Journal of Geography in Higher Education*, Vol.13, pp.85-9.

Kaplan, E.A. (1983), *Women and Film*, Methuen: London.

Karsten, L, (1989), 'Feminist Geography in the Netherlands', *Journal of Geography in Higher Education*, Vol.13, pp.104-6.

Katz, C. and Monk, J. (eds.), (1993), *Full Circles - Geographies of Women over the Life Course*, Routledge: London.

Kelly, L., Burton, S. and Regan, L. (1994), 'Researching Women's Lives or Studying Women's Oppression?', in Maynard, M. and Purvis, J., *Researching Women's Lives from a Family Perspective*, Taylor and Francis: London.

Kelly, L. (1988), *Surviving Sexual Violence*, Polity Press: London.

Khan, N., Saigol, S. and Zia, A. (eds.), (1995a), *A Celebration of Women*, ASR Publications, Lahore.

Khan, N., Saigol, S., and Zia, A. (eds.), (1995b), *Aspects of Women and Development*, ASR Publications, Lahore.

Kitzinger, C. (1994), 'Taking It Like a Man', *Times Higher Education Supplement*, 24 June.
Knox, P. (1991), 'Scholars and Gentlemen', *Journal of Geography in Higher Education*, Vol.15, pp.90-5.
Koertge, N. and Patai, D. (1995), *Times Literary Supplement*, 17 November.
Kuhn, A. (1982), *Women's Pictures: Feminism and Cinema*, Routledge and Kegan Paul: London.
Lauretis, T. de (1984), *Alice Doesn't - Feminism, Semiotics, Cinema*, Indiana University Press: Oxford.
Lerner, G. (1986), *The Creation of Patriarchy*, Oxford University Press: Oxford.
Lewis, A. (1990), 'Interrupting Patriarchy: Politics, Resistance and Transformation in Feminist Classrooms', *Harvard Educational Review*, Vol.60 (4), pp.467-488.
Lim, L. (1990), 'Women's Work in Export Factories: The Politics of a Cause', in Tinker, I. (ed.), *Persistent Inequalities*, Oxford University Press: Oxford.
Lindsay, B. (ed.), (1980), 'Introduction', in Lindsay, B (ed.), (1980*) Comparative Perspectives of Third World Women: The Impact of Race, Sex and Class*, Praeger: New York.
Lloyd, A. (1994), *Doubly Deviant, Doubly Damned*, Oxford University Press: Oxford.
Lorde, A. (1984), 'Age, Race, Class and Sex: Women Redefining Difference', in *Sister Outsider: Essays and Speeches*, The Crossing Press: Freedom, California, USA.
Lorde, A. (1986), 'Stations', in *Our Dead Behind Us*, Sheba Feminist Publisher: London.
Lucas, A. (1984), 'The superior sex?', in *Teaching Geography*, Vol.9, p.234.
Luke, C. (1994), 'Women in the Academy: the Politics of Speech and Silence', *British Journal of Sociology of Education*, Vol. 15, No. 2.
McDowell, L. (1979), 'Women and British Geography', *Area*, Vol.11, pp.151-5.
McDowell, L. (1983), 'Towards an Understanding of the Gender Division of Urban Space', *Environment and Planning D: Society and Space*, Vol.1, pp.59-72.
McDowell, L. (1986), 'Beyond Patriarchy: a Class Based Analysis of Women's Oppression', *Antipode*, Vol.18, pp.311-21.
McDowell, L. (1990), 'Sex and Power in Academia', *Area*, Vol.22, pp.323-32.
McDowell, L. (1992), 'Engendering Change: Curriculum Transformation in Human Geography', *Journal of Geography in Higher Education*, Vol. 16, pp.185-97.
McDowell, L. (1994), 'Making a Difference: Geography, Feminism and Everyday Life - an Interview with Susan Hanson', *Journal of Geography in Higher Education*, Vol.18, pp.19-32.
McDowell, L. and Massey, D. (1984), 'A Woman's Place?' in Massey, D. and Allen, J. (eds.), *Geography Matters!*, Cambridge University Press: Cambridge.

McDowell, L. and Peake, L. (1990), 'Women in British Geography Revisited: or the same old story', *Journal of Geography in Higher Education,* Vol.14, pp.19-30.

MacKenzie, S. (1983), 'Industrial Change, the Domestic Economy and Home Life' in Anderson, J., Duncan, R.D.S. and Hudson, R. (eds.), *Redundant Spaces?,* Academic Press: London.

McLennan, G. (ed.), (1991), 'Politics and Power', in *The Power of Ideology,* OUP: Oxford.

McNast, S. (1993), *An Adult Higher Education,* Leicester NIACE.

McNeil, M. 1992), 'Pedagogical Praxis and Problems: Reflections on Teaching about Gender Relations' in Hinds, H., Phoenix, A. and Stacey J., (eds.), *Working Out: New Directions for Women's Studies,* Falmer Press: London.

McRobbie, A. (1978), 'Working Class Girls and the Culture of Femininity' in Women's Studies Group.CCCS (eds.), *Women Take Issue,* Hutchinson: London.

Magarey, S. (1995), 'Looking at the World through Women's Eyes: One Experience of the NGO Forum on Women, Beijing, 30 Aug-8 Sept 1995', *Australian Feminist Studies*, No.22, Summer, pp.138-154.

Mama, A. (1995), *Beyond the Masks, Race, Gender and Subjectivity,* Routledge: London.

Massey, D. (1984), *Spatial Divisions of Labour. Social Structures and the Geography of Production,* Macmillan: London.

Maynard, M. and Purvis, J. (eds.), (1996), *New Frontiers in Women's Studies: Knowledge, Identity and Nationalism,* Taylor and Francis: London.

Mikell, G. (1995), 'African Feminism: Toward a New Politics of Representation', *Feminist Studies,* Vol.21, No.2, Summer, pp. 405-24.

Mill, J.S. (1983), 'Letter to Alexander Bain, 14 July 1869,' in Stibbs, A. (ed.), *A Woman's Place,* Avon Books: Bristol.

Modleski, T. (1988), *Women Who Knew Too Much: Hitchcock and Feminist Theory,* Routledge: London.

Momsen, J, and Kinnaird, V. (1993), *Different Places, Different Voices. Gender and Development in Africa, Asia and Latin America,* Routledge: London.

Momsen, J. and Townsend, J. (eds.), (1987), *The Geography of Gender in the Third World,* Hutchinson: London.

Monk, J. and Hanson, S. (1982), 'On Not Excluding Half of the Human in Human Geography', *The Professional Geographer,* Vol. 34/1, pp.11-23.

Morley, D. (1980), *The Nationwide Audience,* British Film Institute: London.

Morley, L. (1993), 'Women's Studies as Empowerment of 'Non-traditional' Learners in Community and Youth Work: A Case Study', in Kennedy, M. et al. (eds.), *Making Connections: Women's Studies, Women's Movements, Women's Lives,* Taylor and Francis: London.

Moseley, M.J. (1979), *Accessibility. The Rural Challenge,* Methuen: London.

Mulvey, L. (1975), 'Visual Pleasure and Narrative Cinema', *Screen,* Vol.16 (3), pp.6-18.

Nain, G.T. 'Black Women, Sexism and Racism: Black or anti-racist Feminism?', in *Feminist Review*, No.33, Spring, pp.1-22.

NGO Forum on Women in Beijing '95, 30 Aug-8 Sept, Final Report: *Look at the World Through Women's Eyes*.

Nicholson, L.J. (1990), *Feminism/Postmodernism*, Routledge: London.

Nicholson, L. and Frazer, N. (1990), 'Social Criticism without Philosophy: an encounter between Feminism and Postmodernism', in Nicholson, L.J. (ed.), *Feminism/Postmodernism*, Routledge: London.

Nye, A. (1994), *Philosophia*, Routledge: London.

Oakley, A. (1974), *The Sociology of Housework*, Basil Blackwell: Oxford.

Omolade, B. (1993), 'A Black Feminist Pedagogy', *Women's Studies Quarterly*, Nos.3 and 4.

Orbach, S. (1978), *Fat is a Feminist Issue*, Paddington Press Ltd: London.

Owen, M. (1994), 'Commonality and Difference: Theory and Practice' in Davies, S. Lubelska, C. and Quinn, J. (eds.), *Changing the Subject*, Taylor and Francis: London.

Owen, M. and Price, M. (1996), 'Sitting Pretty?: Women's Studies and the Higher Education Community.' in Elliott, J. et al. (eds.), *Communities and Their Universities: The Challenge of Lifelong Learning*, Lawrence and Wishart: London.

Parmar, P. (1981), 'Gender, Race and Class: Asian Women in Resistance', in Centre for Contemporary Studies, *The Empire Strikes Back*, Hutchinson: London. pp.236-275.

Peake, L. (ed.), (1989), 'Arena: The Challenge of Feminist Geography', *Journal of Geography in Higher Education*, Vol.13, pp.85-121.

Perkins Gilman, C. (1966), *Women and Economics*, Harper Torchbooks: USA.

Perkins Gilman, C. (1981), 'The Grand Domestic Revolution', in Hayden, D. (ed.), *A History of Feminist Designs for American Homes, Neighbourhoods and Cities*, MIT Press: USA.

Pickup, L. (1988), 'Hard to Get Around: A Study of Women's Travel Mobility' in Little, J., Peake, L. and Richardson, P. (eds.), *Women in Cities. Gender and the Urban Environment*, Macmillan: London.

Plummer, K. (1995), *Telling Sexual Stories*, Routledge: London.

Raghuram, S. and Manorama, R. (1995), 'Gendering Development: Issues and Politics', *Economic and Political Weekly*, Vol.XXX, No. 35, pp. 2162-4.

Rai, S. (1996), 'Women and the State in the Third World: Some Issues for Debate' in Rai, S. and Lievesley, G. (eds.), *Women and the State: International Perspectives*, Taylor and Francis: London.

Raju, S. and Satish, M. (1989), 'Gender and Geography: an Overview from India', *Journal of Geography in Higher Education*, Vol.13, pp.102-4.

Razavi, S. and Miller, C. (1995), *From WID to GAD: Conceptual Shifts in the Women and Development Discourse*, UNRISD: Geneva.

Report on Women's Studies Activities in Europe and the Communities of the European Union (1995), Utrecht University.

Report on the UK Delegation on the Fourth United Nations World Conference on Women (1995), Dept of Education and Employment.

Ribbens, J. and Edwards, R. (1995), 'Introducing Qualitative Research in Women, Families and Households', in *Women's Studies International Forum*, Vol.18 (1).

Richardson, R. (1994), 'I've Sailed Upon the Seven Seas - Perspectives on Gender and Race', in *New Era in Education*, Vol.75 (1), pp. 3-6.

Robinson, L. (1995), *Psychology for Social Workers - Black Perspectives*, Routledge: London.

Robinson, V. (1996), 'Heterosexuality and Masculinity', in Richardson, D. *Theorising Heterosexuality*, Routledge: London.

Robinson, V. (1994), 'Theorising Women's Studies, Gender Studies and Masculinity: the Politics of Naming', in *The European Journal of Women's Studies*, Vol. 1.

Rogers, A. (1996), 'A Chronology of Geography 1859-1995', in Agnew, J., Livingstone, D.N. and Rogers, A. (eds.), *Human Geography. An essential anthology*, Blackwell: Oxford.

Rogers, C. (1951), 'Student-Centred Teaching' in Rogers, C. *Client Centred Therapy*, Constable: London.

Rogers, C. (1983), *Freedom to Learn for the 80s*, Merrill: New York.

Rose, D. (1989), 'A Feminist Perspective of Employment Restructuring and Gentrification: the Case of Montreal' in Wolch, J. and Dear, M. (eds.), *The Power of Geography*, Unwin Hyman: Boston.

Rose, G. (1993), *Feminist Geography. The Limits of Geographical Knowledge*, Polity Press: Cambridge.

Rowbotham, S. (1977a), 'Hidden from History', in *Woman's Consciousness, Man's World*, Pelican Books: London.

Rutherford, J. (ed.), (1990), *Identity - Community, Culture Difference*, Lawrence and Wishart: London.

Schild, V. (1995), 'NGOs, Feminist Politics and Neoliberal Latin American State Formations: some lessons from Chile', *Canadian Journal of Development Studies*, Special issue, pp.123-147.

Schniedewind, N. (1983), 'Feminist Values: Guidelines for a Teaching Methodology in Women's Studies', in Bunch, C. and Pollack, S.(eds.), *Learning Our Way: Essays in Feminist Education*, The Crossing Press: New York.

Scott-Clark, C. (1996), 'GCSE Course Wipes Capitals off the Map', *Sunday Times*, 4 Aug.

Sheridan, S. (1990), 'Feminist Knowledge, Women's Liberation and Women's Studies', in Gunew, S. (ed.), *Feminist Knowledge: Critique and Construct*, Routledge: London.

Shrewsbury, C. (1993), 'What is Feminist Pedagogy?', *Women's Studies Quarterly*, Nos.3 and 4, pp.8-16.

Sibley, D. (1995), *Geographies of Exclusion. Society and Difference in the West*, Routledge: London.

Siraj-Blatchford, I. (1994), *Praxis makes Perfect: Critical Educational Research for Social Justice*. Now Publications Co-operative; Derbyshire.

Skeggs, B. (1995), 'Women's Studies in Britain in the 1990s: Entitlement Culture and Institutional Constraints', *Women's Studies International Forum*, Vol. 18, No.4.

Smart, C. (1995), *Feminism and the Power of the Law*, Routledge: London.

Smith, D.E. (1990), *Texts, Facts and Femininity: Exploring the Relations of Ruling*, Routledge: London.

Spender, D. (1990), *Man Made Language*, Pandora: London.

Stanko, B. (1994), *Just Boys Doing Business*, Sage: London.

Stanley, L. (1990), *Feminist Praxis: Research, Theory and Epistemology in Feminist Sociology*, Routledge: London.

Stanley, L. (1995), 'My Mother's Voice? On Being a Native in Academia', in Morley, L and Walsh, V. (eds.), *Feminist Academics*, Taylor and Francis: London.

Steinem, G. (1983), *Outrageous Acts and Everyday Rebellions*, Holt Reinhart and Winston: New York.

Steinem, G. (1994), *Moving Beyond Words*, Simon and Schuster: USA.

Stewart, A. (1996), 'Should Women Give Up on the State? The African Experience', in Rai, S. and Lievesley, G. (eds.), *Women and the State: International Perspectives*, Taylor and Francis: London.

Stone, L. (ed.), (1994), *The Education Feminism Reader*, Routledge: London.

Stone, M. (1981), *The Education of the Black Child in Britain*, Fontana: London.

Tannen, D. (1996), *Talking from 9-5*, Virago: London.

Taylor, L. (1988), *Varieties of Stabilisation Experience*, Oxford University Press: Oxford.

TEST Friends of the Earth (1984), *After the Bus*, TEST.

The Matrix Group (1984), *Making Space - Women and the Man Made Environment*, Pluto Press: London.

Tivers, J. (1978), 'How the Other Half Lives: the Geographical Study of Women', *Area*, Vol.10, pp.302-6.

Tivers, J. (1988), 'Women with Young Children: Constraint on Activities in the Urban Environment' in Little, J., Peake, L. and Richardson, P. (eds.), *Women in Cities. Gender and the Urban Environment*, Macmillan: London.

Tizard, B. and Phoenix, A. (1993*), Black, White or Mixed Race - Race and Racism in the Lives of Young People of Mixed Parentage*, Routledge: London.

Townsend, J.G. and Townsend A.R. (1988), 'Teaching Gender North-South', *Geography Vol.*73, pp.193-201.

Trivedi, P. (1984), 'To Deny Our Fullness: Asian Women in the Making of History', in *Feminist Review*, pp.37-52.

Van Every, J. (1995), *Heterosexual Women Changing the Family: Refusing to be a Wife*, Taylor and Francis: London.

Walby, S. (1992), 'Post postmodernism?' in Barrett, M. (ed.), *Destabilising Feminist Theory*, Polity: Cambridge.
Wallace, M. (1979), *Black Macho and the Myth of the Superwoman*, The Dial Press: New York.
Warner, H. (1993), 'Equal Opportunities: IT and Gender', *Teaching Geography* 18, p.134-5.
Watkins, S.A., Rueda, M. and Rodriguez, M. (1992), *Feminism for Beginners*, Icon Books: Cambridge.
Waugh, D. (1996), *Geography. An Integrated Approach,* Nelson: London.
Weiner, G. (1994), *Feminisms in Education: An Introduction*, Sage: London.
Weiner, G. (ed.), (1985), *Just a Bunch of Girls: Feminist Approaches to Schooling*, Open University Press: Milton Keynes.
Welch, P. (1994), 'Is a Feminist Pedagogy Possible?', in Davies, S. et al. (eds.), *Changing the Subject: Women in Higher Education*, Taylor and Francis: London.
Whitelegg, E. (ed.), (1989), *The Changing Experience of Women*, Open University Press: Milton Keynes.
Whittle, S. (1996), 'Gender Fucking or Fucking Gender?' in Elkins, R. and Kind, D., *Blending Genders*, Routledge: London.
Wilkinson, S. and Kitzinger, C. (eds.), (1995), *Feminism and Discourse - Psychological Perspectives*, Sage: London.
Williams, L. (1987), 'When the Woman Looks', in Doane, Mellemcamp, Eilliams (eds.), *Revision Essays in Feminist Film Criticism*, American Film Institute:USA.
Williams, P. (1991), *The Alchemy of Race and Rights*, Harvard University Press: Cambridge Mass.
Wilton, T. (1995), *Lesbian Studies: Setting an Agenda*, Routledge: London.
Winship, J. (1987), *Inside Women's Magazines*, Pandora Press/RKP: London.
Women and Geography Study Group.(1984), *Geography and Gender. An Introduction to Feminist Geography*, Hutchinson: London.
Woolf, V. (1928), *A Room of One's Own*, Penguin: London.
Wright, C. (1987), 'The Relations between Teachers and Afro-Caribbean Pupils: Observing Multi-racial Classrooms', in Weiner, G. and Arnott, M. *Gender Under Scrutiny*, London: Hutchinson.
Wright, D.R. (1985), 'Are Geography Textbooks Sexist?', *Teaching Geography,* Vol. 10, pp.81-3.
Young, G. and Dickerson, B.J. (eds.), (1994), *Color, Class and Country - Experiences of Gender,* Zed Books: UK.
Young, K. (1993), *Planning Development with Women: Making a World of Difference,* MacMillan: London.
Yuval-Davis, N. (1994), 'Women, Ethnicity and Empowerment', in Bhavnani, K. and Phoenix, A. (eds.), *Shifting Identities, Shifting Racism*, Sage Publications: London.

Zedner, L. (1994), *Women, Crime and Custody in Victorian England*, Oxford University Press: Oxford.

Zhang J. (1994), 'Development in a Chinese Reality: Rural Women's Organisations in China', *Journal of Communist Studies and Transition Politics*, Vol.10, No.4, December, pp. 7-92.

Subject index

abuse 94, 108, 141, 143, 150
alienation 34, 39
assignment 25, 40, 46, 47, 52, 73, 74
BBC 130
biography 8, 15, 69, 90
building societies 4
consultation hours 40
driving licence 57
education departments 97
enlightenment 13, 70, 74
epistemology 1, 15, 18
examination 16, 52, 53, 58, 59, 65, 113, 117, 118, 130, 131, 148
exchange visit 125
fieldwork 51, 52, 53, 55
gender studies 5, 61, 110, 154
healing 12, 90, 92, 93, 94, 95, 96
health 8, 24, 26, 81, 138, 139, 140, 141, 144, 145
homophobia 40, 42, 88, 90
householders 4
industrial relations 134
infanticide 150
interviews 15, 23, 24, 29, 37, 131
lesbian and gay studies 4
liberal studies 5, 118, 120
marxism 70
military service 127
mobility 52, 55, 56
Montessori 131

national curriculum 51
part time contracts 4
partners 6, 26, 27, 142
passive learning 67
pay 24, 133, 135
physical education 131
poster 52
principal lecturer 4
professors 4
questionnaires 23, 24, 29, 42, 59
Ruskin College 118
salacious 108, 109
sample 57, 59, 60, 64, 65
school 2, 10, 30, 35, 39, 42, 43, 51, 53, 56, 57, 59, 61, 64, 65, 70, 72, 77, 91, 92, 94, 98, 120, 121, 122, 123, 128, 131
self recovery 95
siblings 26
skin colour 94
slavery 90, 91, 93, 95
soap box 110
socratic method 118
supermarket 57
survey 6, 52, 129
text books 51, 92
trades unions 4
Worker's Education Association (WEA) 117
xenophobia 40

DATE DUE

			Printed in USA

HIGHSMITH #45230